DECODING GEN Z

BRIDGING THE MINDSET GAP

CLAIRE MOODY
RALPH MOODY

Published in 2024 by Target Training Associates, UK

Designed, Produced and Written by Claire & Ralph Moody

ISBN: 9798321137307

Decoding Gen Z : Bridging the Mindset Gap

If you would like information on our courses and services, contact us on +44 0800 302 9344.

www.targettrg.co.uk

Enquiries to: info@targettrg.co.uk

CLAIRE & RALPH MOODY

In the spirit of gratitude, we dedicate this book to our beloved son and the greatest Generation Z person we have ever met, Jack Moody.

His presence in our lives is our greatest blessing.

We extend our heartfelt thanks to those who have supported us throughout this journey, offering their invaluable insights and perspectives.

CONTENTS

Introduction 7

1. What Motivates Generation Z? 21
2. How to Communicate with Generation Z 37
3. Generation Z and Their Dysfunctions 53
4. How Do We View Generation Z? 83
5. Upward Management and Generation Z 96
6. Generation Z and Technology 112
7. Generation Z: What Do They Value? 128
8. Human Resources and Generation Z 143
9. Flexibility and Work-Life Balance for Generation Z 157
10. Generation Z and Leadership Styles 172
11. Corporate Responsibility and Sustainability 189
12. Navigating Feedback and Recognition in the Workplace 204
13. The Power of Mentorship and Reverse Mentoring 220
14. Generation Z and Personal Development 237
15. The Importance of Diversity and Inclusion 252
16. Summary 268

Afterword 281

About the Authors 283

INTRODUCTION

As you open up this book, eager to learn more about Generation Z and management, we're sure you're probably wondering: why did we embark on this writing journey? How we came to create this book remains our sincere motivation for compiling our own insights and those of so many others from across the industry. The genesis of our book, in fact, lies within our own training courses and what we have experienced as trainers and coaches.

Over the years, we have been blessed with the opportunity to take part in the creation and leading of global training courses. We have worked with dozens—if not thousands, at this point—of professionals across the industries as they focused on how to improve their management and leadership. Even despite their diversity, the differences between their organisations, and even where their primary market resided, we saw some common themes beginning to develop that stood out to us.

So many leaders and managers all had the same qualms and comments, mainly about Generation Z. There was an echo, so to speak, that resonated with us across the globe. Several of our attendees stated that they struggled to understand Generation Z, feeling as though they were trying to manage people who were so different from their workforce. Many even expressed frustrations and shared that they had no idea how to reach them. This was not just across one industry or sector, but across nearly every company, industry, and sector that we encountered.

In other words, there was an apparent misunderstanding and lack of appreciation for Generation Z, and a critical gap that we were curious to solve. The palpable frustration was something we wanted to fix to help companies become more efficient and cohesive; regardless of where they were located, and what their company demographic looked like. Not only due to the emotional responses from our trainees, but also because of what we were hearing.

The inability to understand Generation Z and work with them effectively was creating a ripple effect of challenges. These challenges were costly and vast, signalling a clear need to focus on how we could work with this evolving demographic. There was no time to waste either. As I am sure you're well aware, the growing diversity of the workforce today shows no signs of stopping, as Generation Z is becoming more and more prevalent across nearly every single company and industry. Something had to be done. Thus, our inspiration for this book.

Our purpose in writing this book was twofold: first, to foster an understanding. We wanted to be the messengers of what we know to be highly relevant, critical information. Our goal was to help managers and leaders navigate the ever-complex, diverse workforce that they were dealing with by understanding Generation Z intimately, including their motivations, values, goals, and how they think. Even then, we also wanted to share insights that would help our Generation Z readers, too, to ensure that the connections between generations could be met and momentum could be realised in every organisation.

Second, we also wanted to write this book to facilitate adaptation amongst managers and leaders who are struggling with the complexities of Generation Z. We understand the challenges of working with diverse generations more than you might imagine. Generation

Z, like any other generation, as you will come to find, is distinct and has its own unique traits. However, just as they have to adapt to our ways of leading, we must also find ways to adapt and grow as leaders. Just because we have reached the top does not mean we stop changing; instead, we continue to grow regardless. Our goal was to help facilitate adaptation with confidence based on our findings and to pave a pathway for all leaders to evolve as their organisations do.

With this generation poised to become the dominant demographic in the workforce in the near future—even in the next couple of years—we must all do our part to understand their unique perspectives, as well as their behaviours.

After all, we may be the leaders now, but that is not going to be the same in the next few years, even after a decade. Baby Boomers will eventually retire, and then who will we hand the power over to? That's right: Generation Z, among others. If we want to ensure that we are passing on the leadership to trusted hands, we must first trust them and learn to adapt, too.

To truly ensure that our industries and organisations are left in the best hands, adaptation is necessary. If we don't adapt, our enterprises will not adapt either. As you will come to find, Generation Z is the most entrepreneurial and technologically savvy generation we may have seen yet. If we want to see change, all we need to do is understand who they are, what they value, what they know, and how we collectively can benefit from their expertise.

About Ralph & Claire

We always find this part a little weird so first allow us to introduce ourselves: we are Ralph and Claire Moody, the founders of Target Training Associates Ltd. With a shared passion for training and coaching, we have had the distinct privilege of working with leaders and managers across the globe, delivering transformative experiences to various professionals, companies, and industries. Drawing upon our wealth of experience, we remain committed to facilitating learning and growth for those eager to expand their horizons.

Married for four decades! We've weathered life's transitions together, both personally and professionally, from our early adult years until now. Our journey has been one of constant adaptation and flexibility, consistently underpinned by mutual respect and a shared commitment to progress. We view life as an ever-evolving tapestry, embracing change and seizing every opportunity for growth. It's also what inspires us as trainers, coaches and leaders of our own organisation.

About us from our company bio

Ralph and Claire developed and designed all of the courses that Target Training offers, something that they are immensely proud of.

Before the start of Target, Ralph was in the Royal Air Force and led a successful career where he undertook a variety of operational and management duties, including a role as a training manager and air defence specialist. Ralph believes that lifelong learning is precisely that—something not limited by age or perceived ability and something that we can all engage in to become the best leaders and individuals possible. His philosophy is that limiting belief is what holds the majority of people back, but with appropriate coaching and mentoring, we all can achieve anything that we set our minds to. Specifically, Ralph specialises in training, management and leadership development, leveraging three decades of experience to train today's professionals for the future. Additionally, Ralph is also a proficient, renowned motivational speaker and a keen aviation enthusiast and pilot.

Claire, like Ralph, comes from an aviation background and is an experienced coach and trainer at Target Training, has been part of the company operation since the very beginning. She's the type of person who always goes the extra mile to ensure that value is consistently delivered and people always leave training sessions having learned as much as they could. As a performance coach for the Royal Air Force she specialised in Aircrew and the Air Battle Management Branch, significantly improving performance and pass rates among those taking challenging courses. Passionate about training and coaching, Claire possesses over 35 years of experience in the field and within quality assurance roles. Her expertise with trainer inductions, standardisation, and quality assurance has supported corporate clients all over the globe. She possesses an MSc in executive coaching and is accredited by Ashridge Business School, a world leader in executive coach training and development. She also has a degree in coaching supervision where she enjoys developing coaches. As a qualified pilot, she, too, enjoys flying with her husband, Ralph.

We mean this!

As trainers, our number one goal is to deliver value and to ensure that our book impacts you, your business, and your future goals. With over three decades of experience, we're thrilled to be a part of your organisation's journey and look forward to watching you thrive. Whether you're simply meeting us for the first time or picking up our book after coming to one of our training courses, welcome. We are happy to have you here, and we can't wait for what's in store.

Our Invitation to You

As you open the pages of this book and discover for yourself the insights that we have presented, we invite you to join us on a journey of understanding and adaptation, especially in the context of Generation Z. With so many misconceptions and frustrations; we hope to shed light on what we believe to be an extraordinary generation. This isn't just based on our own son, Jack, who we think the world of, but based on our collective interactions with so many managers, leaders, and employees just like you.

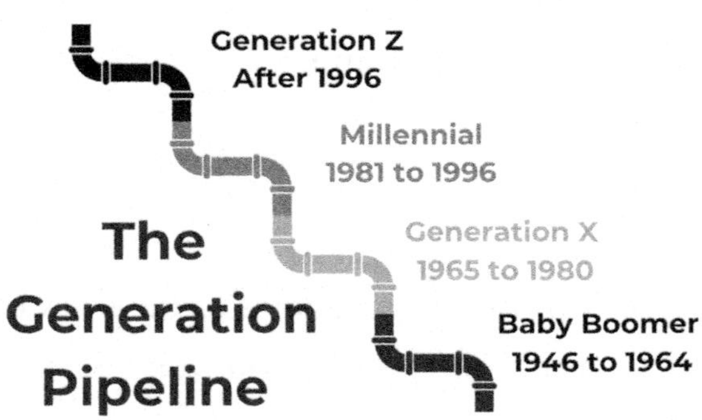

As you can see above different generations are identified within the time period they are born.

Whether you're a Baby Boomer, Generation X,

Millennial, or Generation Z, we invite you to the discussion to learn more about Generation Z. More importantly, we encourage you to consider how we can all adapt. We're not just saying this for ourselves, as Baby Boomers, but also for the entire fabric of our society today.

We are living in an unprecedented time and one of the most remarkable eras in history. As we continue to expand our understanding of the technological innovations that we are working with and developing now, we must come to understand how we need to adapt to the new way of working and management.

Adaptation is critical, and as the old saying goes, change is the only constant. If we reject this change, we'll only be inviting further challenges down the road! We have a clear answer to how we can handle generational differences, and it lies within Generation Z and understanding them on a deeper level. Our need to adapt is universal—whether you're Generation Z or a Baby Boomer like us. And if you're worried about what this adaptation will require, don't be. We're all in the same boat, and we're here to help you comprehend what we can all do to encourage a more prosperous, transformative future for our society.

Together, we can navigate the shifting sands of generational dynamics, embrace progress, and foster understanding. The greatest threat that exists to our future is our inability to accept that change must happen. When we accept that, we can pave a pathway forward that truly does help us all. If we understand the generational differences, similarities, and our own communication preferences, as we will explore, we can bridge the gaps and create understanding.

Additionally, we must also embrace progress. As fellow Baby Boomers, we understand how daunting change—incredibly innovative changes like AI and technology people use today regularly in the workplace—can be. But it doesn't have to be scary. We can take steps to acquaint ourselves with what is required of us, furthering our own comfort in the unknown. The truth is, we have to get comfortable muddling through uncharted territory. We won't know how to go all of the time, and that's okay. But if we embrace progress, we at least know that our destination is a future where efficiency, productivity, and collaboration are expected norms.

By embracing progress and understanding generational dynamics, we can foster an understanding that will be paramount to our organisations. We can say goodbye to frustrations and a lack of comprehension about each other's generations. Our teams can work together, garner further respect for one another, and truly see the power and strengths that we all have—as well as the weaknesses that we can support in one another as we collectively develop and become better professionals.

The possibilities are endless, and we invite you all—regardless of your generation—to take part in this exploration of management and Generation Z.

To Generation Z readers who have picked up our book, we want to extend a warm welcome to you. We are so excited that you wanted to indulge in our insights and learn from our experience. Through this exploration, we seek to deepen our own comprehension of your perspectives and aspirations, paving the way for meaningful collaborations and mutual growth for both of us. This isn't just a book for the older generations to learn from, but a book that I hope we all can gather insights.

Please keep in mind as we start off with our first few chapters, exploring topics related to Generation Z and their mindset, motivations, and more, that what we have presented is our own insights. Based on what we have seen in the industry, as well as our own experiences with fellow Generation Zers—like our son and others—we have presented the chapters of this book as an exploration of our own observations and what we can gather from these examples.

We hope to enlighten you, encourage you to think differently, and inspire you to find commonality amongst those in your workplace. Whether you're a

Generation Z professional or an older Baby Boomer like us, we are so excited to provide you with a look into the future of our workforce and our society.

Together, we know that we can enact significant change as long as we work as a collective group to pursue the goals that we have for our organisations, each other, and even our society as a whole. If you find value in this book after reading it, please share it with others you know would also benefit from our insights.

The more we are conscious of the contrasts and similarities that exist between our generations, as well as the ways in which we can all contribute to being better leaders and managers, the better our world will become.

Our website, www.targettrg.co.uk serves as a testament to our commitment to learning and development. There, you will find a variety of training courses and blogs on management, leadership, and more. Over the years, we have delivered courses and lessons that serve as a means of empowering the leaders and managers of today to become tomorrow's trendsetters and inspirational mentors.

If you are interested in pursuing further support and training to improve your leadership, we would love to see you at one of our courses! And if you have any questions at all, don't hesitate to reach out. We love hearing from our audience and those interested in our work! After all, our ultimate goal is your development and success. We are a 5-Star rated company and that has required enormous dedication and commitment, we believe in what we do.

Join us as we embark on this transformative journey together. We cannot wait to share what we have in store. In the following chapters, we aim to further illustrate the diversity of Generation Z and what they have to offer our organisations if we allow ourselves to be open to adaptation and change.

Remember: adaptation is paramount for our futures.

As you read on, keep an open mind. You'll be impressed by just how much your organisation can do if you're willing to think outside the box and accept the power of what you have available to you.

We hope you enjoy reading this book as much as we did writing it.

Ralph & Claire Moody

1

WHAT MOTIVATES GENERATION Z?

Everyone is motivated by something. Whether it be career excellence, their pay-check, or the ability to contribute to a goal larger than themselves. Motivation is the key to enabling action in any organisation.

In this chapter, we will explore Generation Z and what motivates them. While there are some similarities between Generation Z and others, there are still some distinctions that we—in our opinion—feel are critical to know as a manager.

The first, arguably most apparent based on our observations and research, is the importance of their values and purpose, which motivate them individually and collectively as they contribute to larger projects and teams.

Generation Z is known for having a strong sense of purpose and values, which direct them professionally and holistically in all areas of life. They seek meaningful work and are driven by causes near and dear to their hearts. For example, many Generation Z workers are motivated by social justice, environmental sustainability, and diversity.

More so than others, Generation Z wants to impact the world around them positively. This also means they will be attracted to organisations that align to these goals and values, allowing their work to reflect on their hopes for contributing to the world.

Another primary motivator for Generation Z is the importance of a work-life balance. Generation Z differs from many other generations who have prioritised career

advancement at the expense
of their personal time.

They place high importance on the work-life balance they can maintain, valuing flexible work environments, remote work, and flexible hours. Generation Z likes to have the time to pursue their interests and support mental health, which is not always possible when contributing to the office and commuting daily.

If organisations can offer a better work-life balance opportunity for Generation Z workers, they can capture this demographic and further align with their motivations.

Because of the highly digitised world that Generation Z has been raised in, they are also significantly motivated by technology and innovation. Generation Z are very comfortable and tech-savvy growing up in today's increasingly digital world. They are inspired by innovation in the latest tech trends, always looking at the latest phones, computers, and developments, much of which drive them to specific roles and industries. Generation Z is attracted explicitly to industries and roles where they can engage with cutting-edge technologies and contribute to this innovation.

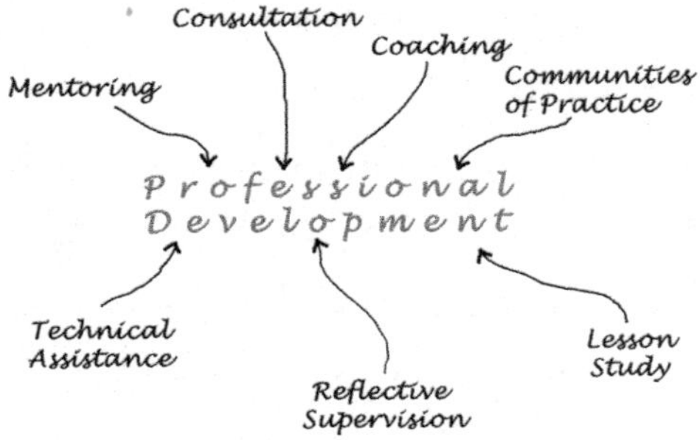

Another primary motivator for Generation Z is personal development. Like some past generations, Generation Z is increasingly motivated by their ability to continue to develop and improve themselves. They are incredibly keen on learning and personal growth, seeking opportunities for skill development, continuous learning, and career advancement.

Generation Z is very motivated by employers who invest in their professional development and provide clear paths for progression. Without this, many generations of employees may feel as though they do not have as many options as their current workplace, leaving them feeling demotivated and undervalued, which is why it's crucial to incorporate opportunities for continuous learning and development within the workplace, especially for those who manage Generation Z employees.

However, perhaps more importantly, Generation Z is increasingly motivated by security and stability. Their desire for flexibility and meaningful work is balanced by the valuation that they put into job security and financial stability.

Because of growing up during economic uncertainties, such as the World Economic Recession and the COVID-19 pandemic, these individuals are increasingly focused on finding opportunities to support them and ensure long-term stability.

Employers in most industries would benefit from providing their Generation Z employees with more long-term support and financial stability, which pair well with the continued emphasis on growing and developing every employee in the workplace.

CONCERNING INCLUSION AND DIVERSITY, Generation Z is increasingly motivated by the presence of both of these in the workplace. As the most diverse generation, Generation Z prioritises inclusivity in all environments.

They value the opportunity to be diverse, to be recognised for who they are individually, and to share their different perspectives without worry of rejection or negation of their perspective. Generation Z benefits the most and is motivated by a strong culture of respect and equality in the workplace, positing that employers who incorporate this into their team environment will benefit and continue to encourage their Generation Z workers to succeed.

FINALLY, perhaps the last quality we have noticed in our research regarding Generation Z is how significantly motivated they are by authenticity and transparency. Honesty and openness in communication, personally and professionally, are crucial to Generation Z.

They prefer authentic communication. They are more likely to be loyal to brands and employers that are transparent and genuine. If your workplace struggles with transparency and open communication, this may be a deterrent for Generation Z workers, further showing the importance of embracing more authentic and transparent communication on all levels at the workplace.

While many of these values and motivators may seem generic, it's crucial to understand every motivator that Generation Z responds to, not only because it will help the workplace but because it indicates how our world is changing and the importance of instant gratification, among other topics.

. . .

We often think how society and social media work is a testimony of how we have developed over the years, but Generation Z has the next level of input. How they think, how social media works, and its format indicate exactly what Generation Z is looking for. Looking at TikTok, for example, everything is only 30-second to 60-second videos, suggesting a short attention span and concise information.

The immediate response that technology drives and the quick responses and access to online shopping are significant factors in our modern society. People have several things available at their fingertips at all hours of the day, every day of the year, regardless of where they are. If you think about it from an employee's perspective, quick results, high expectations for immediate responses, and fast resolutions are paramount, as they are also for consumers. This has undoubtedly shaped how we expect work to be done and how we can expect Generation Z to respond to the workplace.

In today's society, the instant gratification related to getting things done, sometimes without anticipation, is part and parcel of the journey. Still, it's even more critical because technology has influenced this. Technology has arguably driven instant gratification, and we believe that Generation Z is much more in tune with this than previous generations, which is fascinating.

. . .

We believe that the anticipation is the exciting part. If you think about it, it's a lot like receiving presents. You like the idea of the present rather than what it may be. We're not saying that Generation Z does not like this. Still, there are differences due to the instant gratification in social media as opposed to the instant gratification people feel in real life, especially in the workplace.

You have to think that when someone thinks of something these days, they simply type it into social media. Our generation and era sometimes waited a significant amount of time only to be very disappointed by the answer we received. However, the instant gratification we see from Google and YouTube is an entirely different story, further indicating how times have changed.

From the management perspective, sometimes this is recognised but not necessarily dealt with. One area that we have found through many discussions that is needed is appreciation. People enjoy a quick "great job" or a "thank you." More importantly, they also want to know why something is significant, an area often forgotten in feedback and recognition. Just saying something is "good," is not enough.

Many older generations sometimes forget or don't feel comfortable giving appreciation, so they often forget about it or omit it from their speech with other employees. Some people can be highly task-oriented and problem-solving; over their working years, appreciation may not be a key area they think about. It's not that it's not a priority, but it's about getting on with the job and being objective rather than taking time to share feedback, as this took a back seat to other initiatives.

Saying Thank You goes a long way!

In delivering training and facilitation, we have found that youngsters will sit and check the information you are giving them. When training, we discourage this, as it can be a significant disruptor. It's not a problem during coffee or lunch breaks, but seeing this during training is inappropriate. However, what this does signal to us is that they may trust social media for everything, sometimes more than the trainer or facilitator. Personally, we, as baby boomers, find this realisation quite scary.

An example was when one of us wrote something

on the flip chart. One delegate said the spelling was wrong. It was not, but one of the delegates checked it on their phone on Google, looked up and confirmed that we were right! We would have never done this ourselves, but we have to recognise that there is simply a different mindset when it comes to Generation Z compared to us.

We think we have to recognise that generations each trust social media much more, and since they will be a tremendous working force in the future, we need to be more aware of this and how it will impact society. This will move in many directions, so we should all be prepared for the changes. We have not even thought about several changes in social media that will have implications for organisations and employers everywhere.

AFFINITY BIAS AFFECTS US ALL, as it is where a group starts to think as one, ultimately creating what is called "Groupthink". This is where everyone confirms their views based on the perception of the group. If you want to know what this looks like, go to a sporting event and watch it in action, where the supporting teams perform Group Think actions to support their team. Like all generations, Generation Z is capable of affinity bias, just like the rest of us and social media pushes this even more.

Despite some of the challenges with Generation Z and the differences we have pointed out, as a leader and manager, you should build teams with differing points of view and opinions. The best teams have outsiders on their squad. However, a significant danger with Group Think in Generation Zers is that, they won't be challenged, because the group thinks that way.

Every generation needs to get on top of social media. Not because it's the new cutting-edge technology and it's here to stay, but because we have to know what they are looking at and what Generation Z believes. Let's face it: Google can say anything, and it will be believed. Group Think is perfect for the Google generation, and Generation Z finds affinity in this approach.

We suspect that in the future, there will be challenges against social media as it continues to grow and nudge our thinking, but this will not deter Generation Z and others from turning to Internet sources for support. Look at AI, what a huge powerful force this is.

When looking online, Generation Z looks at absolutely everything. They always look at illnesses and sometimes catastrophise everything. A manager or leader needs to think about the issues that this can cause when it comes to wanting things instantly. In the workplace, this is often not the reality, but there are other areas that Generation Z struggle with.

The ability to effectively analyse information and form a judgment.

We believe there is one area that Generation Z struggles with: CRITICAL THINKING.

Because of the instant gratification and things being so instant, the deeper thinking where good problem solving takes place gets completely lost in some of this generation. This is a problem with critical thinking because things are not instant, so they may give up.

But it's essential to not forget that other areas we've

already mentioned, as they prefer to give and receive opinions online rather than face to face, so things are incredibly different for Generation Z and how they communicate and interact with the world around them.

So, instant gratification is a vast area of social media. We must learn that motivation has to be huge, and ownership and appreciation are vital areas that can help Generation Z and encourage them in the workplace. Besides ownership and appreciation, we believe some other vital areas that motivate Generation Z are being purpose-driven and being a part of technological advancements.

Being purpose-driven is one thing that we know for sure they have a strong desire for. Generation Z wants to make a difference. If work is meaningful, they will be motivated. This, of course, aligns with their values, or they may not be as motivated.

Many organisations will say that they have values, but applying such values in the workplace is vastly different from expectations. This is a problem for anyone, but Generation Z won't like it if they feel their work is not contributing to the betterment of society.

Furthermore, as we discussed previously, technological advancements are another primary motivator for Generation Z. Being the digital natives that they are, there is no doubt that they are motivated by technology more than any other means. If organisations can stay updated on technology and allow their innovation to take hold, Generation Z is our main inspiration.

They will, of course, be far more attracted to companies that embrace digital transformation than those that do not. With the advent of artificial intelligence, the world will likely become even more technological, and Generation Z will become the leader in this area. Consider yourself warned, but we could see some fascinating and exciting changes even beyond our lifetimes.

However, another crucial area is personal development. Years ago, many sectors and industries were not as driven to provide areas of personal development. Still, today, it's paramount to the workforce because when you develop your people, they will build your business. Generation Z wants clear pathways for progression and investment but also flexible work-life balance. They place high value on this, as we discuss throughout much of this book.

Generation Z is the most diverse-driven group on the planet, but we expect this diversity to be even more reflected in the workplace. Generation Z is strong because everybody's voices need to be heard. If they don't have a voice or aren't allowed to offer an opinion, they will be less motivated and more likely to disengage from the workplace.

Aside from this, Generation Z also cares significantly about sustainability and climate issues, mainly because they want to prioritise the environment and the protection of such. Because of this, they will seek out companies that are inclusive and prioritise sustainability and environmental concerns.

It's important to consider that these are all generalisations.

Everybody is unique, and everybody's motivations can vary significantly, even within a generation like Generation Z. When we think about it, instant gratification isn't necessarily negative or inclusive with Generation Z; it also affects several other generations. Instant gratification can drive innovation and efficiency, pushing businesses and institutions to respond quickly and adapt to a fast-paced digital landscape. This is not necessarily bad, because it has led to significant innovation and change in society.

We think it's crucial for organisations, managers, leaders, trainers, coaches, and mentors to effectively engage with Generation Z. To do this, we must be better educated, hence the purpose of this book.

For all of us who are not part of Generation Z, we need a mindset shift. We need to stop seeing Generation Z as the problem and understand them better because they are not the issue. We may be the barrier to further innovation and success. If anything, this book may cause some personal reflection within you, which is always a good thing and only further proof of how much we can evolve and change to promote success and satisfaction for all.

Sometimes we need to shift the Paradigm to create a different way of thinking.

2

HOW TO COMMUNICATE WITH GENERATION Z

Communication is a vast area in any organisation and between people in relationships. When ineffective, it can be a minefield. In this chapter, we will explore communication with Generation Z. Given that communication is such a vast area, it would be challenging to cover all of the topics. That's why, we'll focus on just Generation Z and communication and how we can improve this as managers and leaders.

As we typed this chapter, we received a WhatsApp message with a photo of our son and his girlfriend cooking Spaghetti Bolognese together using a virtual platform.

As they cooked, one was in Newcastle whilst the other was in London. They were following the recipe and eating together, we think this is cool and fun. They tend to watch TV together at the end of the evening, working through a Netflix series they chose together.

This is after all of their work and studying has been complete, but even then, you can see the differences in communication between the younger generations and us, as baby boomers.

This is all different from when we were in our early 20s, if not vastly different such as queueing at the phone box with a pocket full of change . But what great opportunities exist once we think about things differently, or if we communicate through different channels? Adjustments are always needed, but considering how we can take advantage of this era, it's essential to leverage the current tools for an even more profitable and streamlined future.

When it comes to phone calls and preferred communication methods, guess what? They are often seen down on the bottom of the list, weird for the older generations but not for Generation Z. They prefer texting or WhatsApp, as these are increasingly easier for them to use. Furthermore, they prefer FaceTime or another online video tools to actual phone calls, demonstrating the significant differences between our generation's communication and the younger generations that leverage these social media platforms.

There's no doubt in our minds that organisations have many WhatsApp groups and communication channels, but it can be a problem if you have too many. If you find this in your organisation, we recommend prioritising them in groups, much like you do emails. This will not only ensure streamlined communication, but will also further allow you to maintain clarity and efficiency.

So, for us, it is clear that managers need to take an opportunity to change their communication style if they haven't already. This is not so much because our current communication methods are ineffective, but because we need to reach the younger generations where they are and through their preferred mediums. The downside is that we must ensure they receive the important messages, especially regarding work and prioritisation, like coming into work earlier than normal.

If these messages are lost in the woodwork, it can be increasingly challenging to maintain workplace efficiency and team efforts.

As we type this, we have our headphones on, which is another big issue to discuss. How do we manage the use of headphones among younger generations? The reason is that focus can be an issue, and headphones can be a severe distraction. Or, for those who have a much more mundane position in their workplace, it can be a nice place to escape to. Regardless, as managers and leaders, we need to consider these concerns and this clearly communicated as what is expected.

SELF-AWARENESS VASTLY DIFFERS BETWEEN INDIVIDUALS, but once the focus goes elsewhere, people have no idea or even the faintest clue what is happening around them. We always see this in the world around us, even outside the workplace. We often see people walking around London, walking out in front of traffic, totally unaware and transfixed to what is playing in their headphones or looking at their phones, rather than what is happening in the world around them.

We think this is terrifying, especially considering the consequences that could arise from such a situation.

Recently, we saw a young lady looking at her phone with headphones in. She walked right in front of a car at a junction, and the car had to brake extremely hard. She walked into the car, did a barrel roll over the bonnet, landed on her feet, and walked along the road as if nothing had happened. She carried on as if nothing had happened and everything was normal! Yes this really happened.

When it comes to the younger generations and the usage of their mobile devices, it would appear that there is no discipline in place. It's really just like a drug, and everyone is hooked on it. Although this is something that can happen to every generation, we see it more frequently with Generation Z due to the fact that they had a digital childhood.

The scary thing to us, is that individuals appear that they aren't aware with what is going on in the world now, and sometimes miss the important things in life, to concentrate on an important post on social media.

"Sometimes you look around and it appears everyone is in a trance!"

A picture taken in a restaurant queue

WHILE THAT WILL AFFECT EVERYBODY, Generation Z are more likely to wear headphones. For those who continue to get their work done and are actively engaged in more, this is not a problem. It's those who disengage and use it as an escape where this becomes an issue.

Now, when it comes to empathy and relationships, technology clearly cannot provide this. You may see a significant struggle regarding face-to-face interactions, especially when they talk about their emotions. Generation Z struggles with communicating their feelings without needing a technological device to be the buffer. They may be happier telling you emotions via text, as many people struggle with correctly articulating and sharing these thoughts in verbal conversations.

Given this insight, how do we have these difficult conversations? Quite frankly, it can be highly challenging. Some members of Generation Z are not used to this. This can be a massive issue with any form of difficult conversation. Based on what we have observed, Generation Z would rather avoid this than deal with the situation. This has been said so many times in our conversations and many organisations, leading us to believe this is a clear trend about this generation and the younger populations.

However, it's important to remember that many generations have issues with this. Hence, it's not just Generation Z. Still, we must remember that everything for them is mainly done over social media, which makes this specific topic and the importance of empathy and relationships even more important. That's because we must find a way to facilitate these interactions and further encourage them to communicate through multiple methods and multiple channels of communication.

We think there are two levels to consider when it comes to management. The first is that Generation Z will not change, so we must because they are the future, and we are here to pass the torch to them.

After all, do we want them to be like us? The answer is no because we don't want them to be exactly like us. We are no better than any other generation, and replicating past generations would be a mistake if we were trying to innovate and move forward into the future.

After all, change progresses society and, ultimately, what allows organisations to continue to grow and develop over many years.

The worst thing we can do is to attempt to convert Generation Z to be like us. As we have discussed previously, we must recognise that Generation Z has a distinctly different mindset. It's a transition at the end of the day, which, of course, is good. We want to change our mindset, and we want to see the world differently. We need to change consistently and grab the opportunity to move forward and adapt to the changing reality around us. This allows us to work with both the positives and the negatives, allowing us to mitigate but also leverage what's available to create a more prepared team for the future.

In any organisation, a workplace induction is

massively important. Inductions should include what they want from you and what you would want for them. Two-way is by far the best way. You need a two-way communication channel to ensure that people hear each other. The chances are that they will be so far ahead with technology and we need to learn from them. Hence, we have reverse mentoring in place. We can help them, and they can help us, paving away where our competencies and skill sets will create innovation and change.

We mentioned using WhatsApp messaging to tell someone when they need to come in earlier or even to communicate with people when they are late. There is no doubt there are benefits to this platform. Still, there are also more appropriate communication channels for different situations.

Regardless of what boundaries or guidelines set, it's essential to create clear expectations of communication and what is used, versus what should be avoided in specific situations.

Setting clear boundaries is vital in induction.

However, even though we may be compelled to set boundaries, we must remember the health and safety rules and their implications in the workplace. This requires extremely clear messaging on issues such as headphones, phones, and messaging. We had one manager speak about how someone refused to remove their headphones, and consequently, they were asked to leave because their actions were a specific health and safety issue.

We recognise, of course, that there could be massive implications regarding wearing headphones. For instance, this could pose a hazard in the event of a fire or another emergency in the office. Additionally, some may want to wear headphones for their own mental health, which is understandable, particularly if they are more self contained.

This is absolutely something that needs to be clear on induction in situations like this. Clear and contracted rules for health and safety should be instated so that everybody knows the boundaries. Not every organisation has grasped this yet; obviously, some are still discussing and working on implementing this in the workplace. We've worked and talked with several organisations over the last few years, which is why this issue has jumped out at us. It's a growing trend, and arguably, we believe every organisation should have rules and guidelines for navigating these challenges.

It is different for every sector, organisation, and even company department. Of course, as we said, health and safety issues pertain to every industry. There will be apparent differences between using headphones or phones or even messaging on planes, trains, and automobiles, or even working in a warehouse.

Regardless, we believe that induction is critical. There needs to be a clearly well-trained process, not just a tick-box exercise process. Clear expectations and rewards should be provided, but the training by good trainers needs to be proficient, to ensure that these clear expectations are met and the rewards can be adequately provided for those who genuinely follow the guidelines.

There should be an active investment into this, not just a video and someone ticking off a form to say that it was watched and the message

was heard. Everybody should be involved in this effort, as it is up to everybody to maintain the workplace's rules and boundaries and the health and safety of the entire organisation.

As we've mentioned in this book, we have to remember that many Generation Z had their first day at work at home working remotely. This is very different from the feeling you get when you walk into a building. When you meet people first-hand, and you're shown the way, there are vast differences in the workplace dynamics and the communication people engage in.

The skill of a trainer and the induction will be essential to get the right balance in questioning to create ownership and Generation Z. Ultimately, the goal should be to encourage them to agree and buy into the organisation's rules. During this process, question technique is essential for ownership, and further facilitates more responsibility and accountability from your employees.

The discussion of WhatsApp needs to take place along with any usage of phones and headphones, as the rules need to be clear in these situations. There are no assumptions when the understanding is there, and nothing is left undiscussed. When this happens, everybody is on the same page and feels that there has been transparent communication across the board.

Above all else, we must remember that people are not stupid, and they will always knuckle down. But losing someone because the rules have not been clear means an absolute waste of money for any organisation, which is why communicating the rules and making this evident to the employees not only saves the organisation's time with further communication but also further drives the entire organisation more trusting, and more cohesive, as everybody understands what is expected of them.

Based on our observations of this generation, we think there are some critical areas for Generation Z, such as preference and communication. First, besides the obvious TikTok and Snapchat, many Generation Z like Instagram as it captures their attention and interests them. The lack of emphasis on phone calls is essential, especially amongst the highly digital generations that will come even after Generation Z.

We must not forget where the visual fits. Generation Z responds significantly well to images, as, let's face it, they have had a lot more screen time than many older generations. They are very visual learners, but Generation Z are used to having images and videos to convey information. However, despite the heavy emphasis on these visuals, don't forget the use of storytelling, as this can create a connection and further comprehension of everything you are discussing with your employees.

Certainly, in all our training, we always encourage storytelling. The more creative you are, the better. The more you authenticate, the better the trust and the more likely generations will seek out these genuine organisations.

However, we cannot overemphasise the importance of being interactive with Generation Z. Based on our own experiences, we think interaction creates the best learning, no matter what you are doing. Together, we have trained in the region of well over two thousand trainers! We know what works. So, how can you engage Generation Z, or any generation for that matter, with interactive learning? The best ways we have found include puzzles, quizzes, or anything that starts a conversation and gets them involved in the discussion.

Besides all these ideas, don't forget the importance

of snappy messages. They have grown up in a world of short-form content that dominates and prioritises the conciseness of messaging. Generation Z prefers quick and easy-to-digest information. And certainly, our motto is making sure that it's fun. Good and light-hearted comedy can resonate well with Generation Z and be more impactful in their learning process.

As discussed in other parts of the book, feedback must be short, consistent, and regular. Generation Z are very socially conscious, so value plays a huge part in this effort. And, of course, we can't forget to discuss the importance of inclusive language. As we know, if you read the chapter on motivation, Generation Z values diversity and inclusion in a much more significant way, certainly more than older generations have.

The key to this is to adapt our style to truly meet the generations where they are. Whether managing, leading, training, or coaching, it's about understanding. They are digital natives, which is essential to remember when interacting and engaging with them in many different environments.

We must always think globally because awareness is vital to people's daily thoughts. When we think globally, we also think about values and purposes that will align even more with our generations and employees.

When you understand Generation Z and how they want to communicate, you can create even more effective relationships, as communication is paramount in any organisation.

Communication is difficult to alter all at once, so any area that you can adapt and change will be one step closer to better communication with everybody, but especially Generation Z.

If you want to truly reach Generation Z employees and counterparts, communication is essential, and it will be the bedrock of all success that your organisation experiences well into the future.

3

GENERATION Z AND THEIR DYSFUNCTIONS

A dysfunctional team

Like all generations, Generation Z also has challenges and dysfunctions that affect them. In this chapter, we'll explore Generation Z and their common dysfunctions in the workplace and how—and why—teams can become dysfunctional.

We feel that we need to explain how teams become dysfunctional from the outset.

Many people focus on maintaining efficiency, but what happens when teams are dysfunctional? What happens when you find challenges in operations, and how do you overcome them? It is an area—a huge area, in fact—that we spend a considerable amount of time analysing. However, a basic understanding of why this happens and how we can avoid and overcome it is essential for every professional today.

We talk a lot about dysfunction in our management courses, but with the added layer of generational diversity, as they collaborate, there can be even more dysfunctions. As we have explored in other chapters, the challenges, and differences from generation to generation may cause challenges. Still, as managers and leaders, it is up to each of us to cultivate stronger team environments and dynamics.

Before starting this topic, we want to address that most teams are dysfunctional due to their very nature. Due to the usual composition of teams, most teams struggle with some form of dysfunction, whether it be a small issue or one that causes huge challenges. After all, we are human beings at the end of the day.

We are each individuals with our perceptions and

habits that potentially cause challenges due to misunderstandings, or our desire, for OUR PERSPECTIVE to be the most regarded.

However, we feel that Generation Z can provide significant input that has an impact, further creating dysfunctionality. Therefore, we must look at this through a critical thinking mindset, ultimately providing an opportunity for further growth and development.

As we have explored before, Generation Z was raised in a digitally centered universe. Their diverse environment significantly influences their approach to teamwork, requiring the integration of diverse perspectives, inclusivity, and the continued usage of technological tools that many of us from older generations simply have not used. Their version of teamwork is far more robust, but also advantageous, because it leverages technology and other values to bring progress to our organisations.

Please remember throughout this chapter that Generation Z, while great at virtual spaces, faces significant challenges in traditional team settings. Comparatively, virtual spaces and traditional team settings often require a different pace of decision-making, one that Generation Z is not primed for. Still, we older generations are ultimately offering a unique opportunity for us to guide them as they navigate the professional world.

While not explicitly discussed in this chapter or book, decision-making is vital for every current and aspiring leader, including those who are part of Generation Z. Returning to the topic of dysfunction, as leaders and managers, we must understand the dysfunctions presented before us. However, we must emphasise where we can significantly impact Generation Z in overcoming these dysfunctions. The first and most critical of the dysfunctions is that Generation Z needs to TRUST their managers and leaders. Without this, the entire team will face significant challenges in operations and cohesiveness.

Trust is essential in any team.

Ultimately, if there is no trust, your team will have a massive issue. Depending on the composition of your group, a lack of trust could be the end of your operational efficiency, or it could be a small issue that can be easily remedied. Sometimes, you need to look and think about the team you are a part of, deciphering what kind of dynamic is present and how this plays into the lack of trust within your organisation. Whether you have a high-performing team or a new team, those who don't trust each other will create a massive problem, regardless of the size of your team or the project you are working on.

While you may think this can be easily overcome quickly, it can cause significant trouble. When there's a lack of trust, especially from our perspective and experience, you don't get to move forward as a team as easily. You may be unable to move forward as a team, putting a permanent roadblock that must be moved in terms of trust. These roadblocks, while seemingly temporary, can create massive challenges and even factions within your organisation that can be harmful to the overall productivity of the team.

THE BARRIERS that exist because of a lack of trust in your team can create separate groups within the organisation. Let's go through an example. If you see a significant lack of trust from many of your younger workers, Generation Z may create a group within the organisation that works independently or as a separate group within the project team. While these may seem beneficial at first, because of the increase in productivity, what harbours division will ultimately create disinterest and even potential disengagement. Before long a silo has been created.

That's why it's so important that we understand Generation Z: once we understand them, we can cultivate cohesiveness and collaboration further, ensuring that Generation Z and our entire team succeed in their efforts.

MANY PEOPLE BELIEVE that it has to come from the employees themselves. However, the effort to overcome a lack of cohesiveness and trust must come from the managers and leaders. The older generations of business leaders need to step up and lead, bridging the gap of understanding to ensure that everybody in the organisation is on the same page. Yet, it's critical to understand that Generation Z also needs to meet halfway, cultivating a connection that will overcome the barriers to best move forward on the same page to work together. Once this happens, trust can be fostered, and operations will run smoothly again.

So, you may ask yourself how we build trust with Generation Z? Regular face-to-face interactions and team-building exercises are the best way to build trust with Generation Z. These can emphasise personal connections that go beyond the digital platforms, not only showing them the importance of traditional team environments but also further ensuring that these team members feel closer to their older counterparts, ultimately learning and collaborating on projects.

This requires, undoubtedly, a bit of extra effort from the managers, team leaders, and even the leaders themselves in the organisation. But you must do so to cultivate trust and overcome existing dysfunctions.

Without this extra effort, Generation Z may struggle to have trust in their leadership and their management teams. Generation Z needs extra effort to cultivate this trust and social interaction. After all, they have based their entire reality on the social media world they live in because they grew up with it. Generation Z has had access to cell phones since seven, sometimes even younger.

This is why we can work together to bridge the gap, encourage their trust, and further work to increase efficiency and understanding for all team members.

The work environment today is so vastly different from say only five years ago. Trust is the number one challenge in any organisation. Due to the pandemic, the hybrid world has created many issues. We have worked with several organisations over the years. Still, recently, the work environment and trust as issues have continually come up, regardless of the sector of the businesses we have worked with, these have been a huge variety.

With more people working from home than ever before or working from the comfort of their own devices, we believe that more work is needed to keep trust. With so many people at a distance, it is difficult to cultivate the trusting atmosphere many organisations enjoyed before the pandemic.

While many may argue it is about getting people back into the office, we believe other methods can be used. It comes down to the organisation's seniors' understanding and learning how to cultivate this change and connect with Generation Z to encourage this positive effect.

BEFORE BEING able to create any change, we must recognise that trust has eroded and that something has changed. This is something that we must look out for in the future, as there is a delicate balance that must be obtained. We must be able to leave people to work independently instead of micromanaging. It was much easier to watch everybody in the office only a few years ago, but it is not as easy now for managers. Attempting to manage workers at a distance can be difficult, but balancing micromanaging and allowing employees to take ownership of their work independently can be even more challenging.

An area that has become clear to us, as professionals, is that managers have been struggling with this area but have not brought attention to it. They have not even addressed this issue with their managers out of fear that they may introduce an issue, they didn't want to address, which reflects poorly on them. There are several reasons why managers may bury their heads and avoid bringing this to the leadership's attention. Still, ultimately, it comes down to a few specific issues that motivate individuals to do so.

We believe it may come down to promotions or feelings that they will not receive empathy. This is all part of Emotional Intelligence also known as EQ. We believe this is an area of change that can be improved. With more awareness and communication about these challenges, leadership will become aware of these issues, potentially allowing them to help implement change that will improve the management inefficiency of the entire organisation.

However, people may also avoid bringing these issues to the CEO or other members of the management team because they feel that they will not be judged fairly. They feel they may be judged because they lack experience, capability, or even the inability to lead. What many people fear is that the lack of trust that their counterparts have in them is not a reflection of the followers but more so a sole reflection of the leadership, and whether or not, they are capable of truly completing the job that they have been assigned.

What all of this proves is that while many people believe that the only gap that exists between Generation Z workers, and management, there is an even more significant gap that may exist between bosses and their managers. As we have discussed many times, any gap in the workplace is a detriment to the organisation and its overall efficiency.

Micromanagement in action.

Regardless of the organisation's communication, we know that Generation Z dislikes feeling under a microscope. They don't like to feel like their managers constantly look over their shoulders. So, there has to be an element of trust, giving people the freedom and flexibility to complete their work without feeling micromanaged. It's important to remember this may not even be just a Generation Z trend, as many other generations may feel more motivated by being responsible for their work, rather than constantly micromanaging.

THE NUMBER one area we have found that builds trust is demonstrating vulnerability, which is especially important for Generation Z. When managers and leaders show that they're vulnerable, it makes them more approachable, more accessible, and above all else, more human to their workers. The problem is that the label of manager or leader has authority linked to it, so many people feel that they must be stoic and without fault, but this is hardly the reality.

Unfortunately, many workplaces have managers who have created a bulletproof barrier. They never demonstrate themselves to make a mistake, and if they do, it damages their reputation and authority as a manager. Therefore, with this expectation, it can be incredibly difficult for any manager or leader to build trust, especially if a worker feels that the leader that they are working for is perfect. As you can see, there is very clearly, and often right away, a transparent brick wall between Generation Z and leaders.

Sorry!

I am just not good at doing this

Therefore, we must work hard to show and talk about the mistakes that we have made. We must work as leaders and managers to make ourselves seem normal, and to set the scene for Generation Z, to see that they can make their own mistakes, as mistakes are opportunities to learn and develop. As referenced a few times throughout the book, all this is about possessing a growth mindset and genuinely leveraging this to develop and succeed.

While you may think this is only for Generation Z, this happens across every generation. Many years ago, the majority would cover up and attempt to look as perfect as possible, avoiding looking stupid or silly. Certainly, this is an era from nearly two or three decades ago. The problem is, in those days, you would have been ridiculed in some cases, especially if you made a mistake openly, so you were forced to hide and block people from viewing your mistakes. Rather than raise your hand, you were forced to be quiet, as mistakes and vulnerabilities were seen as weaknesses.

This can be relative for many, as they think of their school days. All it would take is a teacher or someone from authority to mock you; then, you have a built pattern in your mind not to raise your hand, ask a question, or not try.

We have learned a lot throughout the generations, but still have a long way to go. It's all about MARGINAL GAIN THEORY. We have to make tiny steps moving forward in the right direction. This great theory works exceedingly well, and we use it constantly in everything we do as coaches and professionals.

In a similar capacity, we need to demonstrate building trust. We don't want to be in a situation where we ridicule people for making mistakes or poor decisions. Regardless if you view it as right or wrong, it's irrelevant. We need to build trust and allow Generation Z—and all workers—to feel comfortable coming forward and approaching their leaders and others to create a more cohesive environment.

SO, how can we ensure trust is built in a Generation Z-fueled team?

We have some ideas that we have used that work well in our experience:

EMBRACE VULNERABILITY

The first way to build trust in a Generation Z fuel team is to embrace vulnerability. As a leader, you must be willing to own your weaknesses and vulnerabilities. Every ounce of authenticity you demonstrate builds trust, so be cautious of faking vulnerability or hiding your mistakes and vulnerabilities. This can come across as emotional manipulation. You also should be careful not to be insecure, but rather to stand confident in the mistakes that you have made to exemplify what it means to be a leader; this will inspire Generation Z and further encourage them to trust you.

LEAD BY EXAMPLE

Next, we highly recommend leading by example. You need to demonstrate that it's OK to risk losing face. You need to show humility and admit that you're wrong, which will encourage your team to take calculated risks without fear of repercussions. If they see you making a risky decision, they will feel more comfortable taking chances and pushing themselves further. They won't fear mistakes because they'll understand, based on your example, that it is beneficial to make mistakes and learn.

Encourage Openness

Encouraging openness is also important in building trust for Generation Z fuel teams. You must foster an environment where mistakes are seen as opportunities for growth. If people make mistakes, don't immediately punish somebody and don't chastise members for their errors. Instead, encourage them, congratulate them on their efforts, and turn this opportunity into a learning moment for everybody involved.

Listen and Understand

To truly build trust with Generation Z, you must listen and understand them. You must actively participate in every conversation, understanding their perspective, challenges, and aspirations. You should do this to demonstrate that you value their input and respect their individuality. Listening skill exercises are essential; we have several of them in our coaching and management courses that work really well. This is critical, so we highly recommend paying attention to this because it works, and further encourages collaboration and trust among all team members.

. . .

Provide Support

Building trust also comes down to being a source of support and guidance. As a leader or manager, your goal is to facilitate, not to dominate. If you find yourself in any position dominating, you should step back and empower your team members to take ownership of the tasks and decisions. After all, you are there as a guide to ensure the project goes smoothly, not micromanaging or making them feel like they must do everything perfectly.

Acknowledge Efforts

Building trust also comes down to acknowledging efforts and making sure people feel seen in the effort that they have put forth. You should recognise and appreciate your team's efforts, publicly or privately. When publicly acknowledging achievements and contributions, you reinforce a sense of accomplishment and shared success. However, some workers would prefer this to be done privately, which will still allow them to feel seen and valued in the workplace, especially for some Generation Z workers. This is covered further in the chapter on FEEDBACK.

One thing to remember is that cultivating trust is an

ongoing process. It requires dedication and authenticity every step of the way. As a leader, your actions and behaviour, set the tone for the team dynamic.

However, aside from building trust, another serious dysfunction that many teams have is the common fear of conflict, which is paramount in many teams.

As you know, the old common mistake there, of course, is that there's artificial harmony. Because unfortunately, when conflict is not dealt with, the ostrich effect comes into play.

There is a certain feeling to an organisation where everyone's getting along well, but in all actuality, there isn't harmony. We have seen this everywhere, even in our past organisations, where people appear to be cohesive, but their overall organisation and collaboration are poor.

The reality is, is that the harmony is artificial, it isn't real. Before continuing, we want to clarify that we're not discussing hateful or spiteful conflict. Thankfully, the world has significantly changed in that behaviour is simply unacceptable by anybody in today's workplace. We are discussing more covert challenges, such as misunderstandings or a lack of cohesion in team functionality.

This is relevant to everybody. Generation Z and

their inherent diversity can be a substantial asset. Still, it requires careful navigation to prevent misunderstandings and to ensure cohesion at all stages. We think Generation Z is excellent at faking it and smiling, looking like everybody's getting along well. However, we know deep down that many of them are struggling. Just think about the massive rise in anxiety, especially social anxiety, in this age group. We've discussed this in another chapter, but connecting to this is essential to discuss dysfunction and where it's rooted.

We have been in many organisations, delivered a significant amount of training, and this comes up again and again. However, on the surface level, it would appear that an organisation is getting along pretty well. But when you listen to the people and watch body language, you can see that's not necessarily the case.

We always recommend watching the data that presents itself to the room, mainly because you'll find more information about the organisation than they'll tell you. Reading the situation and what is not being said is key, this does take practice, but evident to see if you really look.

GENERATION Z STRUGGLES if they don't feel part of the team because they feel a lot of empathy and want to be included. Remember: people remember how you make them feel, not what you say. Generation Z struggles with difficult conversations and conflict, and they also struggle with how to deal with it.

Dealing with conflict is essential for brainstorming, problem-solving, and critical thinking, which are necessary skills for today's workforce and tomorrow's leadership team, which will be solely comprised of Generation Z in only a matter of years.

This issue is rarely taught in schools and higher education, so we believe it must be taught in the workplace. All you have to do is look at the insanity sweeping through the West today to see that sheep-like passivity is the new norm, with social and mainstream media serving as both educator, judge and jury.

It is no wonder that Generation Z struggles when things don't go as planned.

Every generation has this challenge, but Generation Z has much more of it. Just think back to these individuals' first days at work during lockdown: opening up the laptop, working with people at a distance, potentially missing a phone call, or even turning their video off.

In the long term, this does not continue to harbour any form of collaboration, but instead, it can create further distance and be extremely unhelpful for team cohesion in the longer term.

We believe communication understanding is key. It's very important to have a conversation about conflict.

To bridge the gap and encourage Generation Z, we must communicate with them and show them why conflict is healthy for the organisation. We must encourage healthy and good conflict, as it can be an incredibly good lever for change. This is based on data we have found by asking Generation Z the following question:

"How do you deal with disagreements, and what is your preferred method of dealing with this challenge?"

While this sounds strange, we have seriously found this works. All you have to do is ask simple questions, and they will help you gain insight into how to bridge the gap. For example, if you ask them if they prefer disagreements via WhatsApp, text, e-mail, face-to-face, or Zoom, you'll know exactly how to deal with this, and how to approach conflicts with them in the future.

Let's not forget that Generation Z is highly accustomed to instant feedback and rapid progression. They might find the conventional rhythms of team projects challenging and slow. However, guess what? We know this feels odd, but you should get a response by using their preferred communication method.

What is there not to like? Even if you get an odd one who regularly likes conflict for change, we have found that Generation Z has responded well to this approach and continues to become even more collaborative.

The other generations may feel this is strange because the old attitude is just to get on with it. The problem is that your way might not be the best for others. And remember: conflict can be good when it's controlled. It can be an extreme challenge and even troublesome for the organisation when it's out of control.

If you haven't built trust, you will not have healthy conflict. You are never going to have healthy conflict if you can't have trust, because good discussion and debate are predicated on the presence of trust and communication, at every stage of the process.

HOWEVER, one point we want to remind you of is that Generation Z may be used to having conflict on social media, where they are comfortable showing their opinion. They don't have the same amount of fear when they comment as opposed to being face to face.

The reality is the most hateful and spiteful content can occur on social media. Why? Ultimately, we believe because there is no outcome and it is easy hide behind a profile. This may be a generalisation, but it's important to consider for some Generation Z , who may feel this way and engage in conflict where they believe there is no outcome, and to avoid because they feel a real outcome face to face.

WE HAVE an interesting story that we can provide you from one of our management courses. During a session, one of the senior managers turned around and told his team:

"I don't speak cry."

The group around the table included a few Generation Z workers, and you can imagine their reactions, especially in their body language. It was incredibly interesting to watch what happened. With different eras and mindsets, it was obvious that there were diverse responses, but this issue needed to be discussed from a different generational perspective.

The team was highly dysfunctional and needed help. What's unfortunate about this organisation is that most Generation Z staff at that location have started to move on.

THERE'S another story with a different management training day, where we discussed displaying vulnerability; this was a massive issue for this particular team.

This was something we were working with the manager on, and we recognised it was something he was not going to do. He even put his pen down and said:

"I don't do this."

He had an apparent old-school mindset. Different generations react differently, so remember that what was taught or even conditioned to us may differ from what was conditioned for others. The team, alternately, was highly dysfunctional, and much of it related to the leadership.

As we discussed at the beginning of our chapter, every team is naturally dysfunctional. We presented two of so many stories that we could have discussed, as we have several more examples that we could impart. We feel that change is happening now, but we must keep going in this direction; education is ultimately the key.

So, let's explore how we can better deal with conflict and encourage this to be a healthy part of our organisations. Remember, we are talking about positive constructive conflict.

. . .

Acknowledge the Productive Nature of Conflict

The first thing that we should do that we highly recommend is to change our perspective on conflict. We must understand that it's not something we can avoid; it's not something we should avoid at all costs. Healthy conflict is when diverse ideas clash, leading to more robust solutions that can change organisations. We must recognise that embracing disagreements is a stepping stone towards progress, not a challenge for us to prove that we are correct.

Courageously Address Sensitive Issues

Next, we highly recommend having the courage to address sensitive issues head-on. We must create an environment where team members feel comfortable bringing up topics they might feel are uncomfortable or worth shame. Getting comfortable with being uncomfortable is something that needs to happen because discomfort should be an opportunity to learn, rather than to feel shame. Shame, being a regular topic in our coaching sessions as many individuals feel shame. When you address these issues openly, you can prevent them from festering, and becoming bigger problems later on, further encouraging more cohesion as a team. The best teams know this.

. . .

Facilitate Open Dialogue

It is crucial to facilitate and maintain open dialogue. Team coaching should be encouraged, during conflict resolution, as this involves skilfully guided conversations to ensure everybody has their voice heard and respected. Remember: everybody is unique, and should be included in these conversations. Team coaching encourages open dialogue and ensures that no valuable insights are left on the table or unexplored.

Embrace Discomfort

We have discussed this briefly, but you must be comfortable with discomfort arising during conflicts. What this does, is to remind your team, that this discomfort is part of the growth process. It is vital that it is approached. When you step outside of your comfort zone, this is where breakthroughs will happen. It's essential to embrace the discomfort, encouraging people to look beyond their perspective, and think deeper about the issues we must solve together.

Harness the Power of Psychometrics

Harnessing the power of psychometrics is another critical tool we recommend in conflict. These can be invaluable in anticipating how team members might react during a conflict situation. But remember: no one way is the right way. These tools can provide insights into personality traits and preferences, helping you navigate discussions more effectively, and foster understanding.

Avoid Premature Closure

One thing that we cannot recommend enough is to avoid premature closure. As a leader, you should avoid shutting out a conflict before it's resolved. Conflict needs time to breathe, and to resolve naturally. If your discussions can be respectful and productive, you should allow the process to unfold organically, instead of attempting to control, or even avoid the heightened tension that arises, that gives way to significant breakthroughs.

Lead by Example

We recommend every leader and manager use their behaviour to set the tone for the team. Lead by example, and show your workers how they should act. If you want them to embrace conflict, you should not shy away from conflict yourself. Instead, model the behaviour that you want to see in others. Show that you're open to diverse perspectives and willing to engage in healthy debates. Your goal isn't to encourage hostile conflict, but rather to foster an environment where disagreements are welcomed growth opportunities. When you utilise these tools and strategies, you'll eliminate a fear of conflict in your organisation, and propel your team forward as a force for change, and encouragement.

Use Conflict as a Lever for Change

If you have the perspective that conflict is a lever for change, then you will be able to change the way that you approach dealing with it. This is a terrific mind-shift dynamic that will further motivate you to approach conflict and continue to see the value of these changes. Seeing it as something positive, extracting a positive from a negative, is a fantastic way to think about it.

The ability to embrace conflict, learn from it, and ultimately harness its power for the development of your teams and organisations is key. Conflict can be a positive step forward on your route to success, thus it is important to embrace it.

Commitment is key

Before we close out this chapter, we want to discuss commitment. One of the most critical dysfunctions we have seen involves a lack of commitment. You should be mindful of this in your organisation.

What's important to remember about Generation Z, is that their commitment to long-term team goals and decisions, may not necessarily mean the same as it does for older generations. We have mentioned this due to how they work in their careers, a stark contrast from the Baby Boomer generation, and others, we have worked with over the years.

It's critical to realise that we live in a fast-paced world, where a social media video may be only a matter of 45 seconds long, and then people quickly move to the next thing. Commitment may appear as fleeting as that, with an evident lack of focus. That means encouraging commitment will be more challenging, but you must do so.

In order to cultivate commitment, it is necessary to include Generation Z in the decision-making process and to discuss the goals that will enhance the vision. Providing them with ownership over the task that they have completed is the most important thing here. This will result in a fantastic alignment with the results, and you will notice a reduction in the amount of dysfunction that exists in the office environment.

In our management courses, we go into a significant amount of detail about dysfunction in teams, we feel this area is one that everybody needs to grasp. We must harness their strengths as we continue to learn and adapt. When we understand and effectively address the potential dysfunctions, we can then guide Generation Z to become more cohesive, innovative, and ultimately productive.

To accomplish this, we need to be honest and confront the dysfunctions that we have. In order to assist us, we need to first examine what we are doing and then perform the necessary inner work. Not only will this ultimately be beneficial, but it will also serve to further encourage our teams and Generation Z to follow suit.

Vital to stop and think sometimes!

SPEND some time thinking about your generation and how you connect with other people, and reflect on those thoughts.

We are curious in the beliefs that you have.

- To what extent are you committed?
- Have you put your faith in your superiors and managers?
- What is your preferred method for resolving conflicts?

It is important to give some thought to the following questions, as the way in which you react to them could play a significant role in gaining an awareness of the issues that we face in the workplace today with Generation Z and other generations.

4

HOW DO WE VIEW GENERATION Z?

In this chapter, we will discuss how we view Generation Z as managers and leaders. We believe it is time to reflect on what we have heard through our training over the last couple of years. This has been a variety of courses in many sectors, allowing us to really gather an understanding of how Generation Z is viewed and some of their similarities. The frustrations that the lack of understanding seems to cause are pretty big, when you look at how Generation Z is seen by many people today.

There is no doubt in our minds, that people's viewpoints are quite different with every generation. Everybody knows this, but things are quite different now with social media and the world of Generation Z; one that is highly technological, as compared with generations of the past.

We have heard so much from older generations and listen to their reactions or observations. The amount of irritation that has been caused and a lack of communication, shows a pretty clear issue in terms of misunderstandings and the potential to honestly not communicate effectively between generations. Most of this, as we have come to find, is due to a lack of awareness, hence why we have written this book.

And we're not just talking about the older to the younger, as we have listened to each perspective. We are also talking about the young discussing the old generations, which we have heard a lot from, and we want to draw your attention to.

Consider this: some really bright and successful people are being groomed for even greater success, and the elder generation is struggling to cope. Something is going on here, as it always has been. But are these issues caused by the Generation Z population, or by Baby Boomers who refuse to understand how quickly things are changing and who will become the workforce's leaders in the next years?

We must recognise that Generation Z is more aware as a result of social media, and they may be well ahead of many of their middle managers from previous generations. Years ago, you would never carry an encyclopaedia in your hand, but now everything happens in an instant.

You can Google something and get the answer in seconds. We older generations appear to be conscious of this, comprehending the enormous power that comes from the tools that we employ now. Interestingly, we do not believe Generation Z is as aware as they may be, given the resources at their disposal.

THINK about some of the comments you've made. How did you describe Generation Z? How did you characterise yourself? I'm sure a few comments stand out to you, but the sad reality is that many have generational attitudes or group everyone together rather than recognising them as individuals.

What we believe and have observed is that something about egos continues to get in the way of people. Some people feel frightened when a specific debate emerges, particularly when it comes to generational gaps and people's attitudes on others. As a middle manager, you may feel uneasy when someone considerably younger than you looks to be advancing over you. It can also spark debate over how much these people know, their expertise, and their lack thereof.

This requires some unpacking; in fact, several of the comments expressed as well as the themes behind many of these complaints must be unpacked. However, not everyone agrees, because some people are more aware of the benefits that Generation Z brings to the workplace. We've heard from several Generation Z members that they have certain challenges, particularly in terms of how others see them, and whether preconceptions accompany them in their professional employment.

What is completely different these days, is that they will simply walk away from the job, because that is how they perceive the workplace, as previously stated. If there is a disconnection, or Generation Z feels ostracised, they will go and look for somewhere else where they will be valued. We believe that many people believe they own their work when they are simply caring for the role and preparing it for the next person who will take it over.

We have to be honest ourselves, and say that over the years, we have definitely felt that. In the past, we have loved the roles that we have taken on, but then, we understand that it is a matter of simply taking care of this role before you separate and move on to the next. It's important to realise that, and we believe there are many individuals who may miss that.

This, of course, affects the older generations, those that have been in these roles for almost 20 to 30 years. This can create irritation for Generation Z, who may feel a lack of mobility in their organisations. They don't want to cause any challenges, but they also don't want to be seen as a nuisance or a hindrance in the workplace. This is especially the case, since they are simply working hard for a company, that they feel aligns with their values and goals.

This all goes back to mindsets, the fixed and the growth, which we will discuss in greater depth in the feedback chapter.

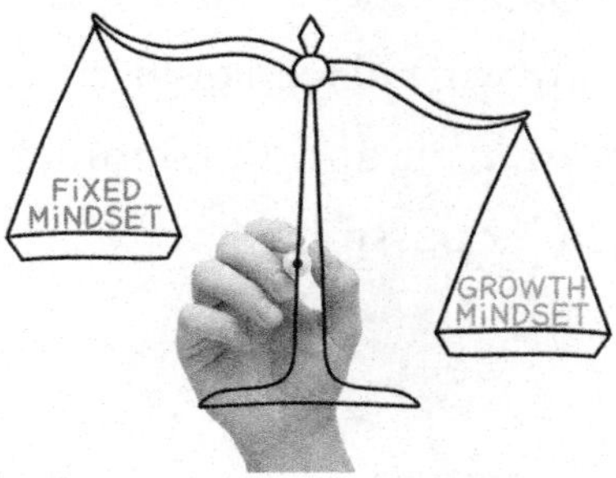

What has been interesting for us over the last couple of years is for those who attend our management courses, the old and bold, who think they know everything, and have been taught everything, often walking away saying that they have learned a lot about themselves. It is a real eye-opener for them to engage in our training and to really explore the current professional world, as well as some of the many challenges that we have seen managers and leaders face in the last few years. Additionally, we have had the same response from the younger generation understanding the older mindset. Some amazing learning has taken place, some real critical moments for change.

This just goes to show you that it is all about education, but it's also about having the right attitude. Having the right mindset is the key in the first place. We think it's because even if you've had management training, and completed it five years ago now, it is already pretty much out of date, so you always need your skills, not only to stay updated, and to be apprised of what the transition in your workplace could currently look like, but to educate yourself and to continue to be the best manager and leader possible.

LISTENING to Generation Z has also revealed to us that some of them have encountered bosses who want to save face and intentionally trip them up. They wait for them to make a mistake because they don't want their ego to be hurt. The managers will then ridicule everyone for what transpired. It is really unfortunate that these opportunities exist, and it actually represents a missed opportunity for connection and true teamwork to ensure everyone's success.

There have been numerous bullying incidences in the past, as well as numerous bullies that have cut down persons in the workplace, and the problem persists to this day. However, there is a substantial cultural shift, as most of the bullying, in its more pronounced form, was typical many years ago but is less prevalent in today's workplaces.

For businesses where Generation Z has had a significant impact, there is a very different cultural expectation, it is one that includes diversity and inclusivity. It's a very different culture than what we grew up with. The old protection, expertise, and unwillingness to admit mistakes. On the other side, the young are open to revealing their mistakes because they perceive them as opportunities to learn, and they don't believe they need to wear armour to protect themselves or their egos.

Keep in mind that we are generalising again, because not every situation is like this, but this is a repeat pattern that we have simply witnessed in our work and the trainings that we have conducted. What we have to remember at the end of the day is the importance of cultural differences. These add an additional layer to how Generation Z are viewed.

When discussing elder generations, we include not only Baby Boomers but also Generation X. We have all grown up in today's world, with its growing cultural and technical context. This can make communication difficult, since certain components of Generation Z culture are difficult to grasp or relate to. However, technology is so huge and immense, that understanding it from a cultural standpoint, is incredibly difficult.

We absolutely respect Generation Z's level of activism and social consciousness. We have heard this a lot from the elder generations. Years ago, we were advised to stay quiet, to be silent, and do our work. Consider how many ideas were held back. Again, it's a shame that we weren't more vocal about the issues and themes that we cared deeply about. So many people held back.

There is a balance in knowing when to be silent professionally, but people held back more back then, whereas individuals today feel more motivated and empowered to speak up. This is typified when Generation Z announce that they are "Speaking their truth".

When we take a moment to reflect on the soldiers who served in the world wars and who went through hell and back, but never spoke about it, we are able to understand where some of this tendency to keep things quiet may have originated. Unfortunately, people were kept back from speaking up, even back then.

We have heard this many times in our training courses, and from the professionals that we have engaged with. So, the older do express their admiration for this area, reflecting on themselves over the last few decades and their own professional experiences.

As we mention in another chapter, the younger generations' engagement with social justice issues and advocacy for positive change, is really seen as a powerful voice in our society today. The generation divide in social media and technology is also covered later.

There is no doubt that older generations view Generation Z as overly dependant on their phones, and there is little doubt that these devices should be used less frequently. However, we believe a balance should be struck, depending on the benefits of such technology. Older generations feel that it is excessive and very different from their own experiences, simply because they did not grow up with as much technology as Generation Z did.

There is still a significant lack of understanding between the older and younger generations, in terms of social media, and phone technology. The problem is the division that this creates needs to be communicated and understood from both sides of the story.

A vast area that we have seen from many older generations is the admiration of the global perspective that Generation Z encompasses. Something that has been driven by social media and has cultivated Generation Z as a demographic. Clearly, it's good to be interconnected and as globally aware as we are today. Especially given the great degree of global challenges, we must be as globally aware as possible.

We feel that it is essential to everybody that they understand global affairs. Of course, this has some negatives, but the positives truly outweigh the challenges. Some do express concern about activism overload, and possible burnout. However, as with all things, there should be appropriate balance, because people should be aware, but also be mindful, of their own mental health and the way that this affects performance. We are aware that the worries this causes, has helped increase anxiety levels among young people.

THEN, of course, the emotional resilience we have talked about is a huge area that we should discuss. This area, many years ago, simply was dealt with by telling people to just get on with it. In some cases, this works, but in some, it definitely doesn't. Just think about the rise in stress and anxiety since COVID-19, which has become such a prevalent problem among young individuals today.

However, there is one central area that older individuals admire about younger generations like Generation Z, and that is innovation. Older populations admire how innovative and resourceful Generation Z is, simply because of their ability to seek and work on their own much more than the older generations can. The different educational upbringings set diverse pathways and levels of motivation in terms of self-starters and resourcefulness.

Many older generations appreciate the fresh perspective of new ideas that Generation Z provides, especially the different ways of thinking that they present to populations. So, when we talk about it being viewed in both ways, Generation Z will tell you what they like about the older generations: the wisdom, the structure, and, of course, the skills experience. What they struggle with is how older generations struggle with change and how blockages affect them moving forward.

On the other hand, older generations like us Baby Boomers struggle with headphones and reliance on phones, seeing this as a potential hindrance when it could be seen as a benefit. What we must learn is that there is no one right way. It's about taking the best from every generation and creating a collaborative approach, that equally benefits workplaces, managers, and leaders.

So, we feel an important step now is to reflect and think about how you can think differently about the other generations. We must admit, after talking to so many generations and age groups over the years, there is a lot of admiration on both sides. Sometimes, we must stop and reflect on that aspect and not the negative and the frustrations that we may encounter.

Something that we have definitely found amusing and really noticeable, is the dress sense when delegates turn up on our courses. Some of the old still come in shirt, tie and sometimes suits, arriving as professional as possible for the training course. We believe there is a time and a place for a suit. On the other hand, the young turn up as is, and are not worried about how they dress in any way whatsoever.

Dress to impress.

But, the judgments and the comments are quite observable. Observing the data between the generations as they sit there, is so important as a trainer. We even catch the subtle eye glances and the looks, which clearly communicate how each person feels about the other. That is for another day, though, and, of course, another book on this topic.

Needless to say, while there may be differences in values, communication styles, attitudes, and so much more, there is also an opportunity for intergenerational understanding and collaboration. There are more of us today, who recognise the opportunity for multi-generational understanding and cooperation. The importance of learning from one another and working together to address shared challenges will be extremely significant in shaping our future, and the professional world that we see our grandchildren experiencing as leaders.

Our take on this is quite simple: Let's communicate more, don't judge, learn, and collaborate. That is the only way to help the next generation become the leaders that they need to be to continue the progress that we once catalysed.

5

UPWARD MANAGEMENT AND GENERATION Z

We have discussed communication regarding Generation Z, but now, we want to touch on upward management next. However, before we get too far into this chapter, let's first address an important reality that we all likely notice in our lives. Different generations—and their generalisations or stereotypes—can often be misleading. It's essential to recognise that individual opinions and experiences may vary. Our stereotypes and ideas about people based on their generation, may also not indicate who they really are.

Yet, some factors and behaviours of older generations bother Generation Z.

Many Generation Z people today feel that older generations resist change. They see many middle to upper-management professionals, struggling to handle technological change, even demonstrating outright resistance to the opportunity to implement new tools in the workplace. This struggle with adaptation to the latest technologies, ideas, and ways of thinking, can certainly be seen, especially in the eyes of Generation Z, as a hindrance to progress and innovation.

On the other hand, it is important to consider how older generations may be frustrated or bothered by Generation Z. We constantly see the prioritisation of innovation, often feeling like our old methods and techniques are no longer acceptable or commonplace. Even despite these hurdles that we must overcome, it's critical to find common ground. Even more importantly, we must find opportunities to learn from one another.

WE BELIEVE that there's certainly something that can be learned from both sides. We must find opportunities to use our shared ideas and methodologies to create lasting change and progress for the older generations, and our evolving Generation Z workers, and employees. In our reverse mentoring chapter, we discuss great educational opportunities from both sides, rather than just one. Everyone can teach each other something, regardless of age, experience, background, or even goals. It would be a shame to reject people's ideas simply because they differ from ours or are daunting.

Nevertheless, Generation Z could educate older generations. These older generations, like ourselves, were thrown into social media without any real training. Much of what we learned—or developed as a skill set online—was largely untrained, and we came to understand social media platforms over time. You can often watch older generations fumble around on computer keyboards, pressing random buttons, to try and get something done. There's a large amount of frustration when it just doesn't work. But instead of leaving older generations without much of a pathway to truly understand how to complete a task online—even on social media—there are solutions.

Education has improved significantly, but the constant technological changes can be a problem for older generations. When we understand how to use a tool, they will change the platform or add more complexity. Constantly feeling that you must keep up—

or that you're destined to struggle in certain areas—can be challenging, and it will leave some people constantly attempting to educate themselves on the best practices for the latest tools, and gadgets.

We believe this challenge is an opportunity for communication between all generations. This is a chance for us all to learn from one another, to benefit each other, and to fill the gaps in people's skill sets.

There's much to cover in this regard, but the key for both sides is understanding and communicating effectively. With communication and compassion for each other's shared challenges, we can think of how to support these differences. The key to any lasting, positive change, is communication.

After we have engaged and discussed these topics with many Generation Z individuals in our lives, we have noticed that many feel there is quite a disconnect due to the values, beliefs, and cultural differences they experience compared to other generations. There are several ways that Generation Z's world differs from the world that, for instance, Baby Boomers grew up in and began to work as young professionals within. However, what does this disconnect do for everyone involved?

Fortunately, with proper communication and a desire to eliminate the gaps that remain between generations, it creates a bridge. However, without appropriate care and communication, this can create a widening gap, that must be addressed; or else there could be challenges.

Without a connection between generations, there can be a growing sense of misunderstanding or difficulty relating to one another. Communication—as we have explored in depth in this book—is huge, but there's a lot to cover. To add to all the psychometric tools and our understanding of how our brain works, we must consider the generations we speak about and their values.

As stated in this book, it's important not to forget that communication with social media is among the most favoured for Generation Z. This generation loves and values their ability to participate in the discourse, and use online tools to communicate with their friends, family, and co-workers.

Another insight mentioned to us is that Generation Z feels that older generations are less adaptable. Their perception of many older generations is that there are more hurdles to widespread adaptation and change. Of course, we are generalising when we discuss this, as some will always be more adaptable than others. However, regardless of how many people genuinely find challenges with adaptation, this undoubtedly causes frustration for Generation Z.

. . .

We think there will be many perceptions, so education and communication are the keys to overcoming these stereotypes to see the truth of the situation. One thing that we know works exceedingly well is coaching, as we have experienced ourselves in our careers. What has become increasingly apparent to us, is that Generation Z's approach to coaching, is much more open-minded than older generations, who still don't quite understand it. Generation Z seems to understand and value the importance of coaching. At the very least, they are open to the opportunity and willing to try it, especially if it will bring further success for them individually and professionally.

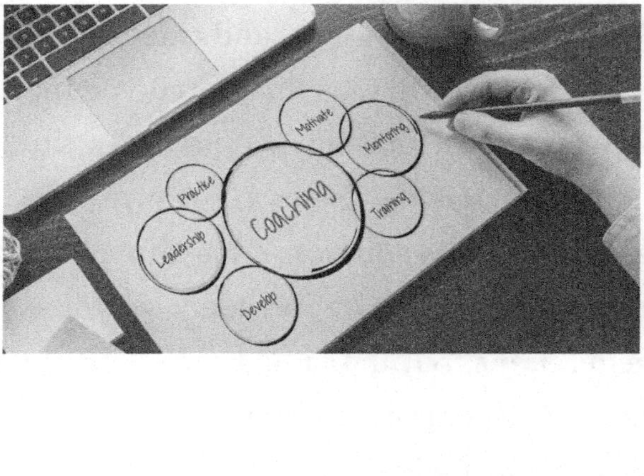

Part of the reason older generations do not have the same perspective on coaching is mainly due to their cynicism. Many of them are more cynical, and sadly, we will hear many older generations commenting, "We don't need any of that nonsense" or "What value does this provide anyway?" The number of delegates who walk away from our coaching courses with a complete mindset change and understanding of what coaching is, and can do, is pretty huge.

For us as professionals, these comments are saddening to hear. However, based on these comments and our own experience, we can understand why Generation Z, will think as they do, about older generations. Even more so, if they hear a comment like this that rejects coaching, before they have even attempted to implement it into their lives, and careers.

Then, of course, there is this stereotype that Generation Z will put all the older, outdated attitudes and beliefs together, giving them a negative view of the older generations. Generation Z has often been viewed as having these collective preconceived ideas about older generations, but individuals are different. Not all Generation Z are engaging in this behaviour, just as not all older workers are like this.

And that, fortunately, is why we talk about upward management and educating Generation Z on how to think about their managers and how to interact in the workplace. Our goal, is to bridge these gaps, allow people to reconsider their previous perceptions of people, and ultimately create an open dialogue between all workers.

Regardless of the points raised so far, building bridges across all generations, understanding and cultivating an open dialogue, and appreciating each generation's diverse perspectives, will help us connect, and eliminate the generation gap. To have more effective workplaces and organisations, it is vital that we at least put effort forth in this area.

So, let's think about managing up and helping both sides: Generation Z and older generations. Upward management is necessary, especially for Generation Z, as they are primed to become the new leaders of our workforce, organisations, and society.

We recognise that this sounds utterly different to

the older generations and those using traditional methods. However, despite how different it is, it is also imperative that we consider the role of Generation Z, and how they influence decision-making, in our organisations and workplaces.

As we will explore in other parts of this book, Generation Z has a strong mindset predicated on a few essential values: sustainability, diversity, and inclusion. These are not new to older generations, but Generation Z has prioritised these, even more so, because of their experiences, and the world they are growing up in.

We must discuss effective communication, which has been mentioned, but also how to build and maintain strong relationships. It is crucial to develop trust and understanding and to learn how to adapt to a manager's style. People should also feel comfortable taking the initiative. With upward management, we can help Generation Z accomplish all of this.

Now, let's be clear: we are talking about management here. Not leadership. Management and leadership are entirely different topics, although being an effective leader will always be a facet of management. To be a good manager, you must be a good leader, but not all leaders have to be managers to make an impact.

. . .

THE REALITY IS that some Generation Z will show natural leadership skills. They may have been allowed to display these skills in their organisations, or they enter the workplace already having these strong traits that make them natural leaders. It can come across as troublesome to those who are uneducated on leadership and management. However, the "troublemakers" you see in the workplace often, have significant value yet to be tapped into.

There are, of course, lots of challenges and workarounds needed when looking at managing up. That is inevitable, but these obstacles are opportunities to create lasting change and to influence the next generation of leaders.

Feedback is a significant part of this. It can help guide your Generation Z workers, looking to improve their skills to become better workers and leaders. In another chapter, we discuss feedback in-depth, but regarding upward management, short feedback and a formal performance review can be helpful here.

As we will mention, short feedback should have a purpose and be beneficial. Even though it may be concise, there should still be thought put into it to ensure your employees' benefit. However, a formal performance review can offer you a more comprehensive assessment of your employees to ensure they see the whole picture. Yet, let us be the first to say that feedback should be asked for and, regardless of one's generation of experience, people should not wait for the manager to contact them. It is up to you to contact, to ask for feedback, and to seek opportunities for change.

This is all part of the growth mindset we encourage people to develop. Having a growth mindset enables you to ask and not fear receiving feedback, whether it is positive or negative. Sure, you may feel that some negative feedback is unpleasant to hear, but with a growth mindset, even a small emotional reaction can be eclipsed by the value that this feedback provides in your growth and development. Ultimately, this mindset shift is up to you. How do you view feedback? Is it helpful, or does it cause you to feel ashamed? Upward management requires communication and implementation of feedback to continue to succeed.

We feel it is crucial to understand, that the ownership can belong to them. Receiving this feedback gives them the responsibility of enacting their change and development. Thus, in managing up, there are some key areas that we feel work the best.

So, as we mentioned ownership, Generation Z will want to feel like they have some influence with their managers. Having a nearly invisible role in their workplace would be unacceptable, as they want to feel valued and heard and value diversity and inclusion. That needs to be communicated, but what a significant step in the right direction.

You should consider what this looks like and when you feel the conversation. The obvious is in our induction phase, as we have seen in our work. We think technology is a critical area that must be specifically mentioned. However, this must also align with the manager and their management style. If you prefer in-person communication, it won't make sense to make a hard shift to technology-based communication. Consider how you manage your team and prefer to lead others, and then implement technology where it makes sense. This also goes for those communicating with managers. Align with their management style, and don't be afraid to adapt to make this more effective.

The classic statement, "not one size fits all," makes sense here. And let's face it: there are so many management styles. We all need to take a moment to reflect on our style, what this looks like, and what needs to be covered in the conversation.

Generation Z want to communicate quickly with their manager, but many may not. Thus, here is the starting point: talking. You can discuss feedback and preferences just like dealing with conflicts. This is incredibly important, not only to you, but to all of the Generation Z in your workplace, to know how to manage in these areas. We don't want to get into Extraversion and Introversion here, that is for another day. There is always conflict and complement sides to both of these. An area that is part of the bigger picture, we deal with this on our management courses.

One of the most expansive opportunities for impact that you could encounter arises when the manager lets their vulnerabilities become known. Therefore, in these instances, trust is built. Remember: this isn't a sign of weakness. This is a sign of your strength to be open and communicative with your team.

Ultimately, Generation Z will be more open to mentorship and opportunities when they realise their managers experience similar challenges. However, they will also be more likely to be interested in mentorship, if a manager shows active interest in them.

As we have mentioned already, we are aligned. Regardless of your relationship, staying aligned and always considering the positives gained from any relationship is essential. The more effort we put forth for understanding, the more benefits will arise.

For our Generation Z readers, we urge you not to gossip at work. It's not natural for everyone, and in some cases, it is better to be professionally silent if the conversation topic could lead to unnecessary conflict. Instead, focus on the outcomes and be clear on how you want to support your boss. The more you understand, the more experience you will gain when entering further roles.

Part of this is also being interested in your manager's interests. Find out more about their passions, hobbies, and what else may occur. This is something important to become less ignorant, as you have an opportunity to build trust, which, of course, keeps rapport.

With all of this said, don't be a pain! It's crucial for anyone, but for Generation Z, we urge you to find appropriate boundaries that benefit everyone involved. Part of this is having emotional intelligence, and understanding when your boss is having a good or bad day. Don't worry if this does not come naturally—not everyone has all the areas of emotional intelligence at a deep level, as many need to develop this over time. The key is, that as you develop these skills, your time, your interventions and ability to know when to approach while showing genuine interest is key.

THERE IS something about being assertive that also benefits people in these situations. As with emotional intelligence, some people find assertiveness natural, while others simply don't. Being assertive is about being in control, using the word "I", and then adding the words you need to get across and communicate to your managers and co-workers. We often get stuck in these situations, but truthfully, we believe we need more assertiveness in people now than ever.

"Being assertive is all about being in control"

ANOTHER CRITICAL AREA of upward management is resiliency and learning to stay calm under pressure. Some can, while some need to work on this, (another part of EQ). Fortunately, this can be taught. Many managers in any working environment should share their skills. There will be a diverse scope of skill sets among many generations, but proper reverse mentoring can create a unique opportunity for education and development.

We have touched upon feedback in this chapter—among others—but it is a crucial area of focus. This leads to further development, and it cannot be skipped over. It must be done well. One problem is that, in the spur of the moment, when you aren't concentrating, this can create a brick wall. We must understand how to deliver feedback to help people understand our message. Otherwise, we may just create barriers between our counterparts.

WITH PROPER DELIVERY OF FEEDBACK, think about the trust that this builds. Think about how much more development and involvement you can create for your co-workers, and employees. Now, when you have a great idea as a manager, ask yourself:

- What can I do to encourage this?
- How can I approach this area?
- What can I do first?

First and foremost, you can allow yourself to be managed from below. Do not hesitate to let your Generation Z workers discuss your management and development. Do this, and you'll watch the trust in your organisation grow even more than you could have ever imagined.

6

GENERATION Z AND TECHNOLOGY

In this chapter, we will discuss generations and technology, a critical area that, if we are honest, feels as though it isn't for us to write about. In fact, we feel that Generation Z should be the ones writing this chapter! However, we ran this past a few of our Generation Z friends and colleagues, many of whom were happy with what we have written.

With that in mind, there is no doubt that Generation Z and technology are shaping the future, primarily through the use of social media. This generation is highly active on platforms like Instagram, Snapchat, and TikTok, even using these platforms to communicate, share their experiences, and stay up to date on current events, even doing so in place of the news.

We all know this, and many of us, mainly the older generations, seem to be playing catch-up when it comes to technology. Well, that certainly is what it feels like. We, of course, at Target use social media as a business, so we are very well aware of the differences in social media use, comparatively between generations.

Also, you have to consider what you use for personal relationships compared to business, because they are very different. Where you want to be seen and how you want to be seen personally and professionally, is quite different. But when you talk to a few different age groups, what is different between Generation Z is that they are given their first smartphone at a very young age. The research says that they get their first smartphone at the age of 12, but our findings show that many of them are given cell phones even well before that. Some of them even by the age of seven!

. . .

Even more importantly, their creativity is pretty unique compared to other age groups. That is why we must understand their knowledge more, hence reverse mentoring, which we discuss in a later mentoring chapter. We have just set up a mentoring programme for another business, as they are the ones that recognise this process and how it can have a positive affect in the workplace.

However, Generation Z, even though they are highly proficient with smartphones, often struggle with more traditional computing tasks.

In many of our conversations with different age groups and sectors, although they are highly competent with smartphones, Generation Z are not good in areas like managing emails, browsers, and more. This was quite common; many said they felt that Generation Z was challenged with these essential skills. We were surprised at that, but quite a few organisations have mentioned this to us, so it is something to note. So, there is something there. It's safe to say that we can't assume Generation Z is comprised entirely of geniuses regarding technology.

We believe it will be down to the individual and their communication style, as this is the key. Communication is, again, pivotal in any relationship or organisation. In these situations, we believe that induction is paramount, talking and making them feel comfortable to show what they know, and in their areas of improvement. This is how you can cultivate trust immediately and ensure a formidable relationship is developed between individuals. This is effective communication.

We must all remember that there may be some pressure here, and that they may not be as good at IT, as people think they are. So, the wonderful peer pressure, covering up weaknesses, is something that we want to nip in the bud from the very beginning. We should aim to encourage courage, build confidence, and allow them to be more transparent.

We also feel you must always ask Gen Z if anything is missing from the induction, certainly review a couple of months down the line. Building and holding rapport is critical because the relationship is the key to any organisation. If something is missing from this vital interaction, trust will undoubtedly be weaker than it could be between others. You are probably realising that induction processes are not just ticks in boxes, they are essential in any organisation and need to be done correctly.

Let's address the time that we all spend on our phones. We think we are a little bit more cautious about the time that we spend on our phones these days. We at Target Training Associates do pay attention to the weekly report. Let's face the facts: it is easy to get distracted. Before you know it, another 30 minutes have passed, and you're drifting away from the task you intended to complete. It is a massive 'time bandit', and here is the reason why our phones dominate our time.

When we check our phones, our brains release a small amount of dopamine. Dopamine motivates us to act, and each time we hear a notification, we check our device. The problem is this dopamine boost is only temporary, and leads to a letdown, which means we go back for more, continuing this process of reaching for the phone whenever we want that little dopamine release. The way to look at this, is that our phones hijack our brains!

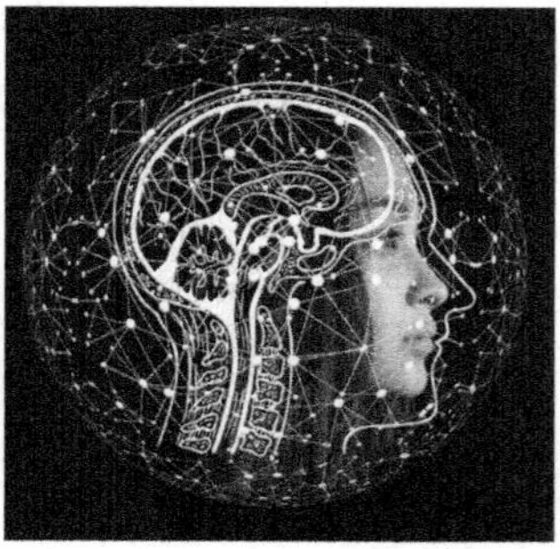

One fact that we found is that some research shows that 55% of the younger generation uses their smartphones for five or more hours a day and 31% of them, feel uncomfortable if they are without their phone, for even 30 minutes or less.

We remember, 8 years ago, walking past a young girl, crying, because she had lost her phone. We thought, why is she crying if she's only lost her phone? But she was distraught, and when we asked her, she explained how she had everything on it, as it carried everything that she needed and everything that she valued. This was before we understood how much information the young carry on their phones, and how valuable this device is to them.

Naturally, since then, we've all probably gone the same way. Let's face it, these days you have to have a smartphone even if you don't want to. That being said, we've met a few people who continue to refuse to own one and claim to be able to function without one. Given the state of technology today, we wonder how long that will last.

Here is a question: do you know what generation has the most internet usage?

It is obviously Generation Z.

Generation Z as a demographic, accounts for the highest user base in Internet usage.

But here are some stats about the frustrations that Generation Z has. Nearly 2/3 of all generations of respondents, almost 58%, claim to spend more time online than they would like to, highlighting the potential adverse effects on their physical and mental health. They are increasingly aware of how being online affects them.

Even so, more than half of all young people, 54%,

encounter technology in their lives that diverts them from their daily tasks. There is no doubt that this is a huge issue, and we have worked with a large number of people on managing distractions, which is a topic that must be addressed due to its prevalence.

Time management is absolutely crucial for everyone, personally and professionally. This is an area that needs to be gripped before it becomes even worse. As it stands today, the overwhelming majority of individuals between the ages of 18 and 24, a total of 69%, say that they use messaging apps more than they used them in the pre-pandemic era.

One area that absolutely needs to be managed, is the continued reliance, on distant messaging and technology to communicate. The young have become so accustomed to messaging as the priority. Older people have reverted back to other communication methods more easily as the habits were formed long ago, so it is more difficult to break these habits.

Think about it, how often do you see young people talking on their phones these days?

What we must remember, is that smartphones have been designed to become addictive, even among older individuals. Many people think governments should do more to control this to help people overcome these challenges.

You must remember the variety of addictions that are possible, often in areas that are not particularly healthy, for example, online gambling. It is pretty sad that many of these addictions continue to this day, as we watch and listen to the addiction that many people have within their smartphones.

We have an obligation, regardless of generation, to watch this challenge. The phone is far easier to use than a fruit machine in a pub, which was the addiction many years ago. This was certainly the reality while we were growing up.

So, without further ado, let's look at the apps, channels, and platforms. Well, the more common ones and the most popular at this time when we are putting this book together. Obviously, with technology moving so fast, the minute you write something, it is immediately out of date. Nevertheless, we'll at least discuss the most popular platforms and apps used today.

Let's first start with the social media channels.

Instagram

Instagram is a highly visible platform, making it ideal for sharing images, short videos, and more. Generation Z loves this app, recites its simplicity, and prefers it for personal branding and networking. Additionally, it allows you to connect within your own social circle.

X (Formerly Twitter)

Generation Z uses X to get real-time news and quick updates. As it provides instant notifications. They value the brevity and ability to engage directly with brands and influencers. Many of them will never watch old-style news channels, for example, BBC. They consider it outdated, so they will get their news from these sources.

Reddit

Reddit is a very popular platform for many generations of users. In this forum-based system, they look for answers to problems that they may have, or contribute to answers for other people looking for specific questions to be answered.

LinkedIn

As a professional network, Generation Z turns to LinkedIn. They utilise this platform for job searches, industry news, and professional development content. This platform has grown for all age groups, as the go-to place for business and one we certainly use.

As you can see, they are the top areas when it comes to social media channels. It's interesting, whatever age group you're in, to consider what you use, how much, and why you value it, much like we explore with Generation Z. This is probably a good reflection time to understand what Generation Z does differently when compared to how they use social media versus how we do.

Let's take a look at messaging apps next. These platforms provide a far more direct and personalised way of interacting. They enable rapid, real-time conversations and are particularly popular with Generation Z. We believe that other generations are becoming increasingly interested in them now that they have seen how fantastic they can be.

WhatsApp

WhatsApp is a popular messaging app that is loved for its simplicity and reliability. It's used for both one-on-one messaging and even group messaging. This is one that we use all the time, as we have lots of WhatsApp groups in our business world, along with other worlds that we are a part of.

Slack

Slack is an app that is used in professional settings to allow for organised, topic-based conversations in teams. Not nearly as popular as WhatsApp, but it sits there at the number two spot at the time of writing this, and one that many companies use and rely on for their projects.

Snapchat

Snapchat is a visual messaging system that is extremely popular with Generation Z, because of its one-time viewing appeal. We have not seen much professional use of this app, but we do understand it to be extremely popular for personal use and communications.

MESSENGER

The Messenger app for Facebook is extremely popular because of its integration with Facebook and its platform, making it easy to connect with friends, family, and colleagues. We think this one is used depending on how much you use Facebook. It must be pointed out that Generation Z does see Facebook as a medium used by older generations!

DISCORD

As an instant messaging and VoIP social platform, Discord allows communication through voice calls, video calls, text messaging, and media and files. Communication on this platform can be private or even take place in virtual communities called servers.

SO, these are the top major messaging apps that are used today. Again, we invite you to take time to reflect on how your generation, over others, uses these applications or doesn't and what you would like to do differently in the future.

LASTLY, let's explore video platforms, a critical area that we believe most people have turned to in today's society. Generation Z prefers visual content, and video platforms cater to this preference. These are some of the most popular ones, which we know, many of you have likely used, both professionally and personally.

YouTube

YouTube is the second most visited site worldwide and a significant hub for Generation Z. This is used for everything from entertainment to education to social media sharing. We use YouTube as we think most generations do, and it's a brilliant platform because of the variety of topics and types of content that are offered.

TikTok

As a video platform, TikTok is well known for its short-form content, and it's prevalent among Generation Z, who appreciate the creative and entertainment value. This platform has grown significantly, and we have found that its usage, is very different in different cultures, making it a very unique platform to explore.

We once stumbled upon some professional TikTokers, which was an eye-opener for us. After chatting with them, we discovered these individuals have millions upon millions of followers. We would have walked by oblivious if we were not nosey!

Claire & Ralph mixing with Gen Z Tick Tockers!

Zoom

For professional and academic meetings, Generation Z often turns to Zoom. Its ease of use, and robust feature, set have made it a go-to for video conferencing. Microsoft teams tends to be more in the public sector, but Zoom when able, is preferred. Let's face it: before COVID, would you have any idea that it would have become as valuable as it is today? We suspect some of you had probably never even really paid much attention to Zoom before. We were not even aware of how brilliant a tool it was, before the pandemic occurred.

For many in Generation Z, they didn't know a world without it.

To summarise all that we have discussed, Generation Z prefers digital, mobile, and visually engaging platforms. They expect the immediacy and appreciate platforms that allow for personalised, authentic expression.

We believe that understanding these preferences is essential for effective communication with this generation. We like to think that things have changed in the older generations, but some people and organisations may still be a little behind. However, it is essential and critical that everyone gets on board with this to understand Generation Z's perspective, as well as the benefits of social media.

As we keep saying, they will become a dominant aspect of the workplace in a short period of time. We need to go forward. What pleases us is that this chapter received a thumbs up from Generation Z—well, from those with whom we shared it, as we needed their feedback to ensure that everything was consistent with their beliefs.

We believe that what we have shared provides a good perspective on Generation Z and their usage of technology, as well as how we might exploit this in the future. We believe we are not far behind, that we are in the right spot, but that we must continue to adapt in order to secure industry efficiency and prosperity.

7

GENERATION Z: WHAT DO THEY VALUE?

Across the generations, different values and belief systems define each individual, but there are some commonalities amongst those of similar ages. Generation Z is one of the most intriguing to study regarding values and beliefs, which is what we will discuss in this chapter.

As we have come to discover, Generation Z has many values that are distinct from other populations. Based on what we have observed, we have no doubt that Generation Z values diversity. This is pretty fundamental in their lives, both personally and professionally, as they have grown up in the most diverse world in history.

Part of the reason Generation Z embraces diversity is that they were educated differently and have a different consciousness than we did 40 years ago, which is obviously a positive thing. The more we understand the benefits and significance of variety, the better it will be for everyone in society, including future generations who may become even more different as time passes.

It is clear that after talking with so many, social responsibility plays a huge part in their mindsets. We've talked about the value of social responsibility with multiple generations of employees and professionals. Generation Z professionals require values, which organisations must convey to them.

Some organisations fail to adapt, which we believe is a preventable issue. Organisations lose a lot of money because they refuse to change. People talk the talk but don't walk the walk, resulting in a massive loss of money because they must continue to attract and maintain customers, frequently without realising what's wrong. We believe that there has been a lack of knowledge in some businesses concerning management adaptability, which we believe is necessary for all generations to succeed.

There is a significant gap in many organisations, despite the fact that there are management strategies that are quite effective in addressing the needs of all generations in the workplace. Many firms provide management and leadership training in a number of formats. Still, there is a distinct gap in comprehending the differences between these generations and how to manage them differently, both above and downwards.

As previously noted, Generation Z emphasises diversity, social responsibility, and work-life balance. They are highly adaptive and, of course, quite technologically smart. These words are repeated because it is what we need to comprehend and what is most important to them. Even if we do not adopt the same habits and principles in our own lives, we must eventually embrace their way of life since, as we have often stated, they will be the future of our professional environments.

Employers who understand and leverage these traits are significantly ahead of the game. This will all play an essential role in shaping the future of work, especially in terms of the changing demographics in value systems, that we will continue to see across all sectors.

Generation Z supports multiculturalism because they have been taught the value of diversity at a young age. Interestingly, this has also been a basic element of prior generations' education, so Generation Z can benefit from it as well. This resemblance can be incredibly effective in connecting with and inspiring emerging leaders.

We've also noticed that Generation Z is more likely to support sustainable practices, environmentally friendly products, and organisations with a strong commitment to reducing their ecological footprint. The importance of sustainability for this generation cannot be understated, as they have become increasingly aware of the importance of protecting the planet.

What's remarkable about returning to diversity, and especially significant to Generation Z, is that they don't discuss it. Diversity is so natural to them that they don't discuss it as much as earlier generations who are still adjusting to this region and the shifting landscape of today's society. Diversity is completely normal for Generation Z, to the point where some of them wonder why it is still a topic of discussion.

We learn so much in the language from our delegates in our courses, and the more aware we are, the more aware we want others to be. We aim to empower people to become better educated about the generational disparities and beliefs that we have identified and take action to address them. We also understand the necessity of tackling issues such as climate change, gender equality, racial justice, and LGBTQ+ rights, all of which Generation Z is deeply concerned about.

It is common practice for us to ask groups to choose their most effective leader in a number of our leadership classes. Generation Z typically names the leaders of modern various fields, frequently referring to them as the best leaders and their role models. Individuals from prior generations, such as Winston Churchill or Alex Ferguson, are frequently mentioned.

It's been fascinating to see how different age groups and cultures describe their best leaders. Their descriptions range greatly, as do their reactions when other members of the group discuss various individuals. It is apparent that there is variance among generations and who we consider to be the best leaders.

What is clear from many of our discussions, is that Generation Z is significantly more vocal about these concerns than previous generations. Their confidence and desire to speak up about certain ideals is a huge topic for them, but keep in mind that we're talking in general terms. This is not to assume that every Generation Z professional will come up with the same level of enthusiasm to speak out on specific topics. We are simply making generalisations based on the bulk of the comments we received, from many of our course participants, and those with whom we have engaged.

When we return to the topic of ethics and principles, there are a few crucial aspects of Generation Z that we need to keep in mind. In comparison to the other generations, Generation Z is technologically advanced, and they are, as we mentioned earlier, tremendously worried about the environment. This is something that we need to take into consideration. In many of their conversations, these are the elements that serve as the foundation. We have found data that suggests these principles have even changed the way that individuals spend, which demonstrates how these values extend both personally and professionally into their activities. This findings are fascinating, because they reveal how these values have affected their shopping habits.

THE REASON that we have observed that the values have an effect on how they purchase, is due to the fact that Generation Z is actually a generation of shoppers who are fairly ethical and who are quite focused on the values that they care about. Despite the fact that they are financially savvy, they are required to do so because the amount of student debt that they have is substantial. This causes them to engage in personal conflicts between ethics and finances.

As a result of financial concerns and the desire for greater stability, they frequently find themselves in a position where they are forced to choose between supporting a company that they believe is in line with their beliefs, and selecting an alternative that is less expensive.

We have to remember that they have witnessed economic challenges like the 2008 financial crisis in their lives, so they have become financially pragmatic. They prioritise practical education and career choices to ensure financial stability and avoid the challenges that they saw in their youth, and even in their early adult years.

For that reason, there may be a lot of inner conflicts that may arise when it comes to ethical shopping and being financially minded. Even despite this, their values are exceedingly strong. We must also remember that they are likely to be on social media as activists, speaking out against companies and people, who may appear to be unethical in their activities.

In situations where individuals have strong feelings about anything, they always share their viewpoint on social media, especially if the group thinks the same way. In contrast to the fact that they are not scared to express their viewpoint on social media, it is possible that they are more reluctant to discuss this topic in person. Having said that, this is due to the manner in which they've grown up with social media dictating.

THERE ARE a few distinguishing features that Generation Z possesses, that can be considered as leverage, despite the fact that many of them have become more comfortable with digital technology and communication as opposed to face-to-face communication, which can be troublesome.

Some reports suggest that Generation Z is more pragmatic and mature than prior generations. We agree with this, and believe it is because they are more likely to attend university and are more cautious about their employment options. To assure stability and profitability, they make the majority of their decisions using a predetermined decision-making procedure.

As it stands, from the baby boomer era, only 3% of individuals went to higher education. Now, that number is 80% in the United Kingdom. This is such a huge difference, and of course, there are positives and negatives to this particular insight.

All the time, we must keep reminding ourselves that Generation Z is different from older generations, because they are the first consumers who have grown up wholly in the digital era. They are tech-savvy, mobile-first, and have significantly high standards for how they spend their time online. They prioritise their time wisely, and it's very evident in what we have seen as professionals.

Many people are curious about how Generation Z and Millennials differ and the other generations. Some even have asked us, "How are Generation Z values different from Millennials?"

That's an interesting area, mainly due to the fact that there are only just a few years between these two generations. First, the main thing to realise is that they are different, and we have to acknowledge that. Millennials appear to be more autonomous and less distracted, but Generation Z is still distracted and confused, but they are significantly more socially conscious and have a greater sense of justice, safety, and privacy than many millennials.

Comparatively, Generation Z is more pragmatic and emphasises direct communication, sincerity, and relevancy. They also place a high importance on self-care, and they are far more prone than previous generations to challenge rules, and authority, since they are accustomed to figuring out what they need for themselves.

We, the elder generations, were constantly instructed to shut up and listen to those who were more experienced and knowledgeable than we were. Generation Z, on the other hand, is accustomed to locating what they require on their own and will trust it far more; sometimes even more than they would trust someone they meet face to face using social media. They also have an even greater global awareness through the prism of social media, which provides both a positive and a negative viewpoint on a variety of issues, that are prevalent all over the world.

Generation Z also has a positive outlook on technology's potential, often seeing it as a valuable tool to solve problems and bring about positive change. They are often early adopters of technologies and innovations over other generations, simply because of their digital savviness. Generation Z likes to gather their findings individually. Let's face it: if we had the same opportunity in digital tools, we would have done the same thing years ago.

In addition, members of Generation Z are significantly more likely to embrace their individual identities and to fight against established stereotypes. As experts working in the many industries, we have witnessed this phenomenon in a multitude of different ways.

As an illustration, in the fashion industry, people seek to demonstrate that they have "no fear" of being different. Almost forty years ago, this was seen to be going against the system and was looked down upon with a great deal of disapproval; but, in today's world, it is welcomed with open arms. Because of the choices they make in their lifestyle and the presence they maintain online, they are lot more individualistic and proud of this.

And as we all know, the short attention span that gets talked about can be extremely positive for them. What we mean is that they are accustomed to quickly digesting content, and can elucidate the meaning of content relatively quickly.

We have to remember that there was a shift in the approach to how Generation Z learned. They prefer diverse learning methods or may even lean more towards online courses, self-directed learning, and hands-on experiences. Lifelong learning is seen as essential in a rapidly changing world, which they wholeheartedly are behind. Comparatively, online courses could be extremely difficult for older generations, who may perform better when in person.

Fortunately, we have found a balance of face-to-face training, backed by coaching calls for a period of time and short focused videos, to be extremely effective at communicating messages to these generations. Yet, when it comes to learning, there are different learning styles to address. We like to think that a combination of face-to-face, videos, and calls is the best method for all generations, even for generations and their short attention span.

Having a short attention span might be seen as a positive trait. It is possible to effectively manage Generation Z if we capitalise on their talents and use them to our advantage.

According to what we have learned, the following is something that we recommend:

Embrace Diversity

Gen Z values diversity in all aspects of life. To manage them effectively, ensuring that the workplace reflects a diverse environment that respects and integrates various cultures, ethnicities, and backgrounds is essential.

Highlight Social Responsibility

Organisations that commit to social responsibility will attract and retain Gen Z talent. This includes being proactive in social issues and having corporate practices that align with their values.

Adapt Management Techniques

Understanding the generational differences is crucial. Gen Z requires a different adaptive management approach that can understand their unique perspectives.

. . .

Leverage Tech-Savviness

Gen Z is highly adaptable and tech-savvy. Employers should leverage this by integrating technology into the workplace and allowing Gen Z to utilise their digital skills.

Support Work-Life Balance

Work-life balance is essential to Gen Z. Management should support flexible working arrangements and respect personal time.

Promote Sustainable Practices

Gen Z is likely to support environmentally conscious organisations. Adopting sustainable practices can be a significant factor in managing and appealing to Gen Z employees.

Encourage Ethical Practices

They are ethical consumers, and this extends to their work. Companies should align with ethical practices in all aspects of business, from supply chain to marketing.

. . .

Understand Their Financial Pragmatism

Gen Z has grown up in an era of economic uncertainty. They are financially pragmatic, so offering financial stability, practical education, and career paths can be appealing.

Acknowledge Their Social Media Influence

On social media, members of Generation Z are vocal about causes that are important to them. Pay attention to and appreciate their online presence as well as their opinions.

Recognise Their Unique Identities

Gen Z resists traditional stereotypes and values authenticity. They are individualistic, which should be reflected in how they are managed and engaged at work.

Utilise Their Short Attention Spans Positively

They are used to quick, digestible content, which can be a positive trait if harnessed correctly, such as through micro-learning and varied learning methods.

. . .

INCORPORATE DIVERSE LEARNING METHODS

Gen Z may prefer a combination of learning methods, including online courses, self-directed learning, and hands-on experiences. Blended learning approaches, including face-to-face, videos, and calls, may be effective.

WITH THE COMBINATION of these practices, Generation Z can align with their values, and organisations can continue to support them and encourage further retention of these vital professional leaders.

It's important to remember that Generation Z is distinct, but there are also individual differences that we must account for. However, on the whole, many of the values that we have discussed are true to this generation, so it's crucial that we understand what they value, how we can meet them, and how we can best support and align with the future leaders of our society.

8

HUMAN RESOURCES AND GENERATION Z

When it comes to Generation Z, one of the major areas that we often overlook that needs to be dealt with, is how we start thinking critically and differently about human resources. Human resources have to deal with every generation, every employee, and every team. However, when it comes to Generation Z, there are some major differences with human resources practices that we feel need to be discussed.

As Generation Z enters the workforce, human resources professionals face the challenge of adapting to the unique needs and preferences of these digital natives. Born into the world of rapid technological advancement, Generation Z employees bring a distinct set of skills, expectations, and work styles. To successfully integrate this generation into the workplace, human resources have to embrace and leverage their digital fluency.

However, at the same time, they must address their desire for meaningful work, flexibility, and a strong company culture. The interaction of all of these unique concerns requires a multifaceted approach for human resources, to truly leverage the power of these individuals from this demographic.

Human resources has had to adapt its recruitment by leveraging social media and digital platforms. Generation Z will only look for job opportunities online. They're not the type to go door to door, and it's becoming more and more apparent as more generations enter the workforce. They have to focus on areas Generation Z considers important, specifically their values.

One example of this is offering flexible work arrangements or even allowing for further career development opportunities. Inclusive workplace culture is another major concern that human resources professionals will likely see, as they refine and improve their recruitment strategies.

It is crucial for us to investigate this and to really touch upon it because it is very important in regard to human resources as a subject. All of these areas have been concentrated on in other portions of the book, but it is essential for us to study this. In light of all of this, the department of human resources has been forced to make a change and completely refocus its attention.

Focus is a keyword here for any human resources or learning and development lead. Basically, it means paying particular attention to the centre of the area. This is the focal point, the major priority, and what these professionals are aspiring to improve.

As Generation Z enters the workforce, HR professionals face the challenge of adapting to the unique needs and preferences of these digital natives. Born into a world of rapid technological advancement, Generation Z employees bring a distinct set of skills, expectations, and work styles. To successfully integrate this generation into the workplace, human resources departments must embrace and leverage their digital fluency while also addressing their desire for meaningful work, flexibility, and a strong company culture.

Human resources has had to adapt its recruitment,

leveraging social media and digital platforms. Generation Z will only look for job opportunities online. They have to focus on the areas Generation Z considers important, for example, flexible work arrangements, career development opportunities, and inclusive workplace culture.

THE HR ROLE is always going to be challenging, having to adapt between the Millennials, Baby Boomers, Generation X and Generation Z, probably, without knowing who is who in many cases.

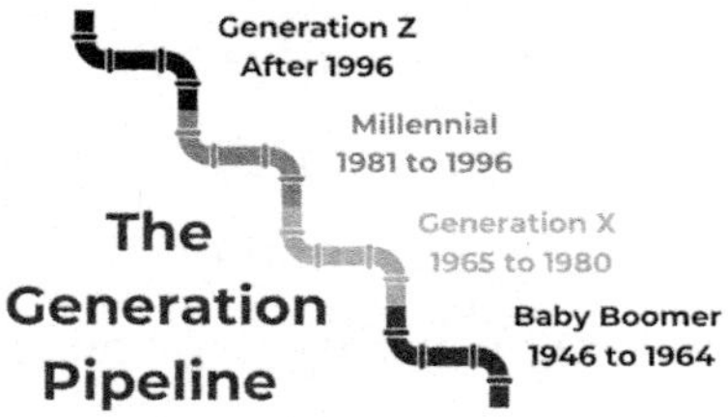

Overall, these four generations have generalised differences that are critical to understand and be able to navigate. Add in the myriad of government policies, and you have an absolute minefield for them to battle.

Furthermore, there are even slight differences between all these generations that we discussed. Millennials often seek a balance between work and personal life, which human resources have had to adapt to, and emphasise, to really understand the importance of well-being for their employees.

As Millennials are native to the digital market, technology has also been an area where human resources have had to adapt to these processes, including onboarding, communication, and performance management. They also appreciate collaborative work environments, so open office layouts and team-building activities foster a sense of community and further engage them in the workplace. Millennials are also highly sociable, so human resources have had to emphasise corporate social responsibility and the values that Millennials believe in.

Baby Boomers are different from Millennials and Generation Z. They value stability and a traditional career trajectory. So, human resources have had to focus on structured career paths, clear hierarchies, and long-term employment relationships.

Human resources, when it comes to training and development, provides more traditional training programs to assist them. Baby Boomers appreciate recognition for their contributions and value loyalty above all else. They also like benefits and retirement packages as they approach that area in their life, so this is another consideration that human resources has had to adjust for, as an example.

Taking all of this into consideration is merely an illustration of how varied the roles of learning and development and human resources are in the workplace.

So, how is Generation Z viewed in the context of human resources?

First and foremost, we have to look at the recruitment process. Here, Generation Z is very wise and quick to learn. Human resources will be wary of using ChatGPT to sift through applications for jobs. It has been known that smart Generation Z applicants use this to write "Hire This Applicant" and then paste it into a text in white, and therefore invisible to the naked eye, so it gets picked up by any artificial intelligence being used to short list applicants.

This is then a code embedded in ChatGPT to say hire them. By the time this book is published, there will no doubt be so many more tricks out there, so human resources has to be very careful in regards to artificial intelligence and the implementation of such and the recruitment process.

If you need a refresher, Generation Z is comprised of individuals who were born after the year 1995. As members of the first generation to have grown up with the Internet, they are born into the digital age. In addition, they belong to the generation that is on the verge of becoming a large portion of the labour force. And this is the reason why we, as managers and leaders, require comprehension.

In particular, in order to make the most of the power that these digital natives possess and to guarantee that the workforce continues to be stable and productive, managers and leaders need to learn about, and acknowledge, the changes that are occurring within the workforce that they have not previously been aware of.

Employers who recognise the importance of mental health will attract Generation Z workers and keep the best of them. They will take a proactive stance on wellness, including changes in how companies treat employees. Health takes priority for Generation Z in literally every area.

Human resources also recognises that Generation Z employees believe that they are more than just their jobs. They want their employers to know the same. However, they have indicated in many polls that they are prepared to work hard even on the weekends and evenings when necessary to develop their careers and achieve security. So, in essence, they are willing to work hard to achieve goals, but they also want to have the balance of choosing when to step away from work and having time off as stated in contracts or even in their job description.

In summary, human resources had to focus on the following for Generation Z:

1. Generation Z is expected to work with modern technology.
2. They prefer in-person interactions (75%, according to the latest research) and feedback from people in real time and in person.
3. These individuals are entrepreneurial, used to technology, and quite savvy in understanding creativity. Nearly 14% already own a business, and 58% say they will own one in the future.

4. Generation Z is less tolerant of authoritarian environments. Having grown up in collaborative environments where they can share their thoughts publicly and receive feedback online, they expect to be heard, and to have their opinions count.
5. Generation Z embraces change more than any other generation in our recent history.
6. They value flexibility, and work-life balance motivates them. They are drawn into roles that offer flexible hours and childcare and value perks, like healthcare, over free food or happy hours.
7. These professionals are competitive, having been raised in one of the most competitive educational systems. They are used to having their work assessed and graded, and they expect this in the workplace.

As you can see, there are huge differences between the generations. Generation Z has been a whole new area for human resources to learn from. Generation Z has forced many human resources professionals to change their strategies and focal points, from their different values, to their entrepreneurial spirit.

Some of the effective strategies for managing Generation Z in the workplace have already been mentioned. Still, to summarise, they want ownership in their career, to be aligned with their values, to work with the latest technology, to prioritise their mental health, and to enjoy a work-life balance.

Generation Z wants to have control over the direction of their career and to be aligned with each value they maintain. With technology moving as fast as it is, Generation Z leverages the tools that are available, even thriving in hybrid environments as they have, for many of them, had to start to work through the pandemic, working in the kitchen on a laptop, or, even in their bedroom, so it's all that they know. This requires unique strategies that human resources professionals need to take advantage of.

Unquestionably, a great number of problems that are negative have been overlooked or lost, and they are the kinds of problems that can be handled as we get to know the generation better.

In our business world, we have developed coaching programs that are proven to help. In some cases, we have focused on coaching Generation Z differently than any other generation we have worked with.

When it comes to coaching, we have found that

Generation Z responds so well to one-on-one coaching. It can be face-to-face, or online, and they respond even better to external coaches. It provides them with a safe and trusted environment, rather than working with someone potentially in the workplace, that they feel may not be the best fit for them, and their needs.

Many businesses now have internal and external coaches. The generations that exist inside your business require coaching in a variety of ways. It is difficult to apply a single answer to all generations. We are not referring to training or mentoring, but rather coaching. All domains are quite distinct, with various skill sets and expectations for achievements. Coaching is a vast area of expertise, with numerous approaches.

Some major companies have taken it upon themselves to leverage Generation Z and their strengths. Some companies, in our opinion, are much more proactive than others. They have taken these steps even as leaders in their industries, the first to do so, to truly take advantage of what is available to them. They have noticed and seen the opportunities and grabbed them.

As we have explored the world of Generation Z in depth, we have learned to take some of their advice in some key areas. As Baby Boomers, there are some differences between our generations. Some of these have been really exceptional to recognise as we focus and then think about what we can learn from each other. After all, to really pave the way for a more progressive future, we have to learn and focus and adapt.

In our opinion, some organisations are trying to push their way onto their employees. There is so much adaptability that can come once we all communicate. Hence, we focused an entire chapter on communication, as communication is so essential to organisational efficiency in itself.

We truly have the chance to learn so much from each other. That is, after all, why we created this book. We wanted a way to bridge the connection between our generations; to understand what we can use from one another, to truly become the best professionals and the best individuals possible. In so many organisations, where we have delivered training, this topic of generations is raised in every training session. Many people are beginning to realise how important it is for us to really come together, and understand the generational differences that exist between all of us. But more importantly, how can we use these differences, to really pave a better pathway forward?

So, leaders and managers, if we are all open and honest with ourselves, we can learn so much from the Generation Z world and what they have experienced in their short lives. We know we have, just as trainers and professionals. The only difference is that managers must first recognise what an issue is, and how big it is. Then, action is needed as early as possible with an appropriate solution.

We believe it is a huge issue when managers try to manage Generation Z. But they only manage them the way that they know, which, of course, is how they were managed and what works for them. The problem is, this doesn't work. Applying what one person, especially yourself, responds best to, is not always the way that you're going to reach other people.

We have to learn what is needed. We have to recognise what is beyond ourselves, and what other people require, in order to truly grow and develop as professionals.

Adapting our human resources practices to the needs of Generation Z is vital for attracting, retaining, and even engaging the student generation of talent. By understanding our unique characteristics and preferences, especially those of others, human resources can create a work environment that not only appeals to Generation Z, but also enhances the overall productivity and culture of the organisation.

When this is done across every organisation and every industry, imagine the ripple effect this creates, and the change that it will influence in the sectors, and across our professional world.

This adaptation is not just a response to generational change, but a strategic move to harness the potential, of a digitally savvy, purpose-driven, and collaborative workforce.

If we do not take advantage of this opportunity to adapt, learn, and genuinely comprehend each and every difference that we maintain in comparison, we will miss out on the possibility to actually evolve and become even more sophisticated and equipped for a more progressive future. In the field of human resources, passing up this chance would be a serious mistake, which is why we urge that we all do our part now to prepare the road for a more empowered, holistic solution that satisfies the demands of every generation in the businesses we run.

9

FLEXIBILITY AND WORK-LIFE BALANCE FOR GENERATION Z

When it comes to Generation Z, two of the most essential values that they regard are the importance of flexibility and a work-life balance.

In this chapter, we will explore this in-depth, considering why they value this, why it's essential to them, and how organisations can meet this need, and still find efficiency in the workplace.

So, what do we think work-life balance and flexibility mean for Generation Z?

After many conversations with various people from Generation Z, it was obvious that the key is, that they want opportunities to have choices. For us as Baby Boomers, our days were always solid working days or hours, where you were at work all the time. Of course, things have changed, and this mindset definitely has changed. In some ways, it's definitely for the better. It simply is a matter of different worlds and expectations.

What we found increasingly interesting is that, when we asked our son about this, he said, "Why would you want to work a nine-to-five, when you don't need to, every single day?" We honestly cannot argue with that. Our son couldn't wrap his head around the idea of the old style of working. He even said that sometimes, you couldn't get anything done at work, because of being constantly interrupted.

This is undoubtedly true, of course, but some people like that, and some don't. It's a matter of the classic extroversion and introversion differences. It's about learning to deal with, and control distractions, which is different for everyone.

With their great knowledge of social media, Generation Z understands the hybrid way of working, much more profoundly than we do. They do not understand why we had to sit at work on the quiet days, when there was no need, similar to how they feel when forced to do the same.

Many years ago, we remember sitting and staring at the clock, waiting for five o'clock to arrive because it was so rigorous. It was sometimes referred to as a bell, to notify us that you may finally go home. That was crazy! This highlights the importance of developing a positive work attitude, as it does not contribute to workplace motivation.

Alas, the flexibility of working hours is what they want. But then again, most generations would like this approach. Many see the value of choosing when and how to work, rather than being forced to sit for a set number of hours a day, especially if there's nothing to do. Because of this, many organisations have implemented this to some capacity.

It's important to note, though, that different sectors have different opportunities available regarding flexibility. Not every company is going to exercise flexibility in a similar fashion. This is, of course, becoming a lot more apparent after the pandemic. Significant changes have occurred for many generations, but for Generation Z, this is all that they know in the workplace. They can only read about what we once did, or listen to their parents' conversations, about what the workplace used to be like, before the pandemic.

We believe, we will never actually go back to the same five days of working every week, especially if it does not need to follow this format in the future. As we say, different industries and sectors will dictate different things, and distinct expectations of what flexibility looks like for workers. As Generation Z becomes more dominant as an age group, in the working field, we imagine this will only change as they implement more of their values across management in organisations.

But then, this also ties into our chapter on mentoring and reverse mentoring. This is a vast area, especially when relating this to networking. The hybridisation of work, and the lack of strict work hours, are going to change how networking is done, and it already has. Networking is done more often on social media, but you can't beat the face-to-face interactions that help people understand each other more deeply.

We believe that some networking has to be split into first-stage and second-stage contacts. There's a way that we will hybridise all aspects of the work environments, and operations, even in the context of networking and mentoring.

We feel that the most important thing to focus on is developing relationships online. However, keep in mind that building these relationships online differs from face-to-face conversations. Different methods are required in these situations, and we had to learn them because this is an unfamiliar territory for us as Baby Boomers.

But you can make it work well in your favour. You have to put in the time, regardless of whether you are online, or face-to-face. Even with different strategies, the amount of time and effort required, still dictates, how fruitful these interactions are for your professional development.

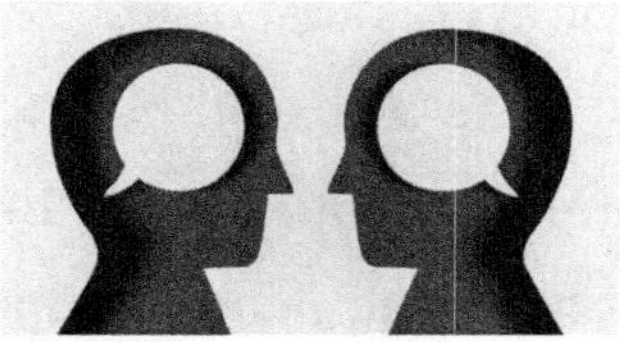

As most people are aware, relationships are the most important aspect of almost any organisation. We believe, however, that following numerous meetings with organisations and on our management training courses, they are suffering with this far more than they may publicly admit. As trainers and professionals, we have noticed a tremendous mismatch between CEOs and the challenges that managers face.

Of course, in the midst of all of this, let's not forget about the short attention span that comes with Generation Z. However, it has become clear that there is a substantial difference with Generation Z. Social media has exacerbated many people's inability to concentrate, particularly among this age. However, keep in mind that we are discussing a broad topic. Not every Generation Z member will have a short attention span, as others may exhibit similar traits to us as Baby Boomers or even subsequent generations.

As a result, both online and in-person interactions must account for a limited attention span. It will be a challenge if not managed properly. Our concentration, and attention span, differ greatly while communicating online versus in person, which must be considered in practically any workplace engagement or even networking. Of course, many businesses manage video-off in different ways today. We are not going to go into the research figures here, but there's plenty to read about it.

Even with all of this said, we do believe the technology is a fantastic tool, and can be used to really maximise the potential, that every organisation and professional has.

Another topic we like to discuss is difficult conversations, and how we learn to work with others, even if we don't like them or communicate with them remotely. Being online allows people to avoid these situations more. In the short term, this may appear to be a positive position for avoiding confrontation, but in the long run, it is completely ineffective.

As we covered in our communication chapter in more detail, we discussed how WhatsApp, e-mails, and text messages can send messages incorrectly or with the wrong intention. What can be seen as a positive e-mail from the sender, is often taken as quite the opposite of the receiver, posing critical challenges in communication and comprehension. Some people are more specific and objective, but this can be slightly blunt.

In all these chapters, it's like a swinging pendulum. Every topic we explore crosses over, and we have to mention some things twice, because of the relevance to each and every topic that we are exploring. We need to explore each situation, including the specifics that relate to both, as you will find that these discussions are multifaceted rather than singularly focused. If we miss these opportunities to bridge connections, our understanding of Generation Z may not be as in-depth and applicable as it could have been.

When viewing all this at a distance, everyone needs to consider all of these factors when building a workforce or adapting to the changing workforce. Some will embrace this new way with ease, but others won't. That needs to be managed of course. Even with people going to work three days a week, the old way brings a whole set of different problems and, of course, some positives.

I won't touch upon the anxiety that this can bring, as this is a vast area to deal with. With the generation behind Generation Z, we need to be even more aware of their well-being, coaching, and mentoring that may be required and will be required to ensure their efficiency, engagement, and effort in the workplace, as valued team members.

Let's face it: social anxiety is huge, but it's just one of the many anxieties out there. There are several different ones that people struggle with all around the world. But social anxiety is the biggest, and it happens to be on the increase.

This is one area that has massive impact on our coaching courses, everyone has or knows someone with this problem, so the conversations get very deep, very quickly.

From comments like, "I don't want to pick up the phone because I don't want to talk to someone, so I will text them," to "I don't want to disturb them," we recognise the commonality of many people's shared experiences when it comes to social anxiety. Many people simply don't like talking on the phone. However, as we've always said, and as the classic statement goes, LEARNING TO BE COMFORTABLE WITH THE UNCOMFORTABLE, is important for growth and development.

In this case, Generation Z has a much different journey. Their well-being is different because they've had to sit at home with family and pets, sharing workspaces, which can create a stressful environment for them. Going to work years ago was a break for many individuals, allowing them to truly focus on what they were doing, and not worry about what was happening at home. The number of times we have heard people say, "Thank goodness I'm here to get away from screaming kids" is much more than you might imagine.

However, during the pandemic, the kids at university had to sit in their rooms alone to eat their food. They weren't even allowed to eat together as a group. You know, that sounds like mental torture and simply being in prison. We believe that this adversity would have made them stronger, in some ways, but sad in others. The human interaction missed.

They will develop new behaviours as a result of this encounter, which will become more obvious. Some behaviours may even be eliminated, while new ones will be developed. However, this is entirely dependent on the companies and unique team environments, and how they develop as a result of these societal shifts.

With all of this said, we think Generation Z, and their life balance, will be better than some of the older generations. We are prime examples here of how our perception of work-life balance is much different from Generation Z's.

Comparatively, they value their time off more, as we

all do, but they simply prioritise it better. Baby Boomers were buying houses when they were twenty. Generation Z will have almost no chance unless they come from wealthy parents. They are all stacked with student debt, something our generation never had to deal with. That is, their mortgage is effectively in their twenties but it is not a mortgage. It's pretty shocking for many of us, in the older generations, to see this happening to the younger ones.

In some cities, you have to ask how anyone, especially a young person, can actually afford to buy a house in these times. The reality is, not many of them can, so it's a very different world that they are living in, and we must respect that. Even if we can't understand it, we must see that their journey is much different than ours was, when we were younger.

Without formal coaching or mentoring, in the workplace, an accountability partner can be extremely handy for this generation. It's an excellent opportunity to think about building the proper habits in people. The right ones, of course, will be determined over time and as appropriate per individual, team, and organisation.

As trainers, we don't think you have to worry much about Generation Z not taking up coaching and mentoring because they're used to sharing their vulnerabilities and will be much more open to doing so. They have not grown up in a world where you must stay quiet, talk when asked or told to, and to keep your opinions to yourself. Again, it's important to remember that we're thinking generally here, but this is a common trend we have seen amongst many of this generation.

In our experience, Generation Z is much more open, and they understand more about coaching and mentoring. They are less reluctant to get involved, happy, and open to growth, and pursuing their goals.

Our talks, and even some in-depth interactions with managers, reveal that they blame Generation Z for workplace issues. Often, it appears to us in some situations, that they have not gone out of their way to adapt. They haven't attempted to understand where generations have come from, when these disputes occur. Some managers appear to be trapped doing the same thing again and again.

This sense of 'stuckness' means managers manage everybody similarly, and stick to what suits them. This area is easy to fix once understood, because it's easy to make changes, once the changes are apparent, to the person causing these challenges. However, at the same time, it's much easier for some to bury their head and ignore the changes, that are slowly happening around them.

CHANGES NEED to be made to management training so that it takes into account all age groups. Once more, the most proactive businesses that we have observed have already understood this concept entirely. Unfortunately, not all of them have, which means that as a result of people walking away, this is such a catastrophic loss of money. This is such a waste.

It comes down to management and ensuring everybody feels valued and supported. Here's a recent example of why we believe this is true. Recently, we were in Graceland in Memphis. We saw a young man sitting in his chair at Graceland at the entrance to the Lisa Marie aircraft. We were so excited to visit the site as keen aviators, as the aircraft was at the top of our list of attractions to see in America!

As we approached the young man, he was concentrating on his phone while wearing headphones. He was paying no attention to anyone who was entering the attraction, and was not even checking tickets. He was completely uninterested, and chose to focus on his phone instead of paying attention. To tell the truth, he required a good old kick up the bottom, if we are being completely honest with ourselves. In what part of the world was the manager?

We also saw numerous security officers in a popular UK supermarket chain who were on their phones and did nothing to prevent shoplifting. They were distracted by their phones rather than carrying out their jobs. Even in these situations, it is the managers' responsibility to deal with it while also efficiently managing others.

As we always ask, where is the manager when you need them?

WE KNOW we've drifted slightly from the main topic, but it's vital information to discuss. Work-life balance, what work looks like, and the flexibility required for Generation Z are huge. To be honest, they're huge for every single age group that we encounter.

One thing that we do love about Generation Z is that they always look to the future. They don't seem to dwindle too much in the past, which we have definitely picked up on in our interactions.

So, a work-life balance to them means not bombarding them with e-mails after work, which is an area that needs to be disciplined. To Generation Z, time off simply is, time off.

In our work, we have examined different strategies to understand Generation Z, and this is what we have come up with. Obviously, flexible hours and goals are a must. Generation Z is acclimated to goals as it has gotten used to the education system. If they don't have them, it creates confusion, which is typical for them.

Generation Z also must have breaks due to short concentration times, so encourage this in the workplace. Always offer support and be prepared to listen to them. Communication needs to be clear and open.

Generation Z also wants professional development, lots of learning opportunities, and to truly feel a sense of fulfilment in all they do, personal and professional.

They prioritise work-life balance more aggressively than their predecessors, often influenced by witnessing the burnout experienced by Millennials and Generation X. They seek meaningful and fulfilling work but not at the expense of their personal time and mental health.

Moreover, Generation Z places a strong emphasis on mental health and well-being. They are more likely to advocate for mental health days, support in the workplace, and environments that foster psychological safety. For them, a job is not just a means to an end but an integral part of their identity and life satisfaction.

They desire employers who recognise the importance of mental health, provide support for personal development, and offer opportunities for growth and learning beyond traditional job roles.

Providing a proper healthy work-life balance is beneficial not only for Generation Z but also for all employees. It increases productivity and morale and even lowers turnover rates.

So, this concludes our subject of work-life balance and flexibility. We've touched on some of the most important topics we've identified. We hope that these thoughts and insights have helped you learn more about generations, and how we can build a stronger business by managing and supporting their values.

10

GENERATION Z AND LEADERSHIP STYLES

Leadership is a critical area to discuss, regardless of the generation that you are focusing on. In this chapter, we will explore Generation Z and their leadership styles. We felt this chapter was absolutely essential to understand Generation Z and what their vision of leadership is.

We will not be discussing leadership or management because these are entirely separate topics. This chapter is more focused on helping you understand how Generation Z perceives leadership, which may be an important area of insight for managers in any business or organisation.

SIMPLY PUT, Generation Z prefers a more collaborative and supportive leadership style. We believe you would have already worked that out, especially if you notice what Generation Z responds to in the workplace. That is why the coaching approach works for them, most of the time, when it comes to change.

Based on our experience, there is no doubt that the coaching style works for Generation Z and is the one that they respond to the best.

It is undoubtedly a modern approach, and its success is without question. But let's look at how Generation Z view some of the other styles of leadership, that we may exhibit, or even exercise ourselves in the workplace, as managers and leaders.

Transformational Leadership

When we first consider transformational leadership, we will see that it focuses on the inspiring and motivating actions, that leaders can engage in to inspire people to succeed. This resonates with Generation Z. They value leaders that provide a clear and exciting vision for the future, and motivate them to grow and develop their skills.

Transformational leadership accomplishes exactly that. Of course, every leadership style has limitations and constraints, but rapport and connections must remain top priorities. When transformative leadership is offered, Generation Z will feel tremendously involved and have ownership, as you can see from the previous chapters.

Autocratic Leadership

This may make you consider how Generation Z would react to an autocratic leadership style. In any case, there are distinct variances in the leadership styles of different generations.

Those who favour a more autocratic leader are contrasted with those who favour a leader who is more hands-off. There is no such thing as a correct, or incorrect leadership style; nonetheless, certain styles are more effective, when dealing with people of different generations.

Let's face it: the autocratic style is typically adopted during a crisis, and it is one that we, as older generations, would have been more familiar with.

The issue arises when it is utilised all the time. You must delve deeper into the individual, understand them, and tailor your style to their needs. The autocratic style will not appeal to everyone, so it, like any of these leadership styles, should not be applied as a one-size-fits-all strategy.

We think the Baby Boomers probably respond better to the more traditional hierarchical approach, whereas Generation Z, may prefer a more collaborative approach with leadership.

The issue is that many baby boomer leaders have failed to adapt to new leadership styles. As a result, they try to lead and manage in the same way they were led and managed in the past, which obviously does not work in modern times. As a result, several challenges arise within organisations.

You have to keep in mind that this is what we were raised with; we spent a significant amount of time in an atmosphere where this was considered to be the norm. In the case of Generation Z, things are not exactly as straightforward as they may appear.

This brings us to our next leadership style: the democratic leadership style.

Democratic Leadership

Let's take a look at democratic leadership. Generation Z also really appreciates this approach, because it values everybody's opinion, in the decision-making process.

After all, Generation Z wants everyone to feel valued and their contributions to be properly recognised. THAT IS HOW THEY FEEL and feelings are high on the agenda for Gen Z.

They believe that the situations they encounter are handled effectively. They prefer a world in which everyone can contribute and voice their opinions.

It will be really interesting to see how they develop as leaders. Generation Z has the potential to become exceptional leaders, thanks to the innate characteristics, we have discussed in this book so far.

We also feel that organisations should invest in training Generation Z, as managers and leaders, to lead teams and businesses as soon as possible.

There is a lot to learn in this subject from both sides of the argument. Many previously unexplored sectors will emerge, providing chances for growth and development for both leaders and generations.

This is truly an exciting opportunity for everybody! Now, let's move on to the next leadership style.

Authentic Leadership

Authentic leadership works well with Generation Z, which values genuine and honest communication. Generation Z values trust and open support, therefore this model works well for them.

It also matches much of how they view the workplace, and how they view organisational efficiency.

As said in the dysfunction chapter, Generation Z loves authenticity. They seek opportunities to serve while being loyal to themselves and their convictions. So, as a manager or leader, if you catch yourself saying, "Generation Z are so difficult to manage" or, "We don't want any more Generation Z", which we have heard a lot of as trainers over the last couple of years, stop and take a look in the mirror.

YOU MAY WANT to ask yourself if there are any changes that you can make to help improve the situation. Over the past few years, we have seen some managers unwilling to change and meet Generation Z halfway, which undoubtedly hinders the beneficial hidden potential, that is possible if managers are willing to adapt for the future.

Both parties must work to improve their understanding. There is no blame

in this situation, thus we should avoid taking advantage of any opportunity to blame others. We say, "Let's educate". It's an opportunity for both of us, the elder generations and Generation Z, to come up and explore our differences and how we can work together.

When it comes to mentoring, Generation Z will respond to it, so it's important as a leader or manager to take this role seriously and prioritise it. As we have mentioned throughout this book, Generation Z is eager to grow, and with their view on professional development, mentoring is critical for them in the workplace.

It's important to remember that you will be a role model for them. Of course, the critical question is, what type of role model you want to be seen as. How do you want to present yourself to Generation Z, and what kind of workplace do you see in the future? Do you want them to lead for themselves?

When feedback is done correctly, Generation Z will respond and grow with the correct guidance, as we discuss in our feedback chapter. Feedback, along with what they call servant leadership, which means leading by example, and showing how you value the team's well-being, and success, is instrumental in how Generation Z develops professionally, into the leaders they are working to become.

So, without question, role models and mentoring are essential for Generation Z, and are roles that everybody, as a manager or leader, should take seriously. It's your chance, after all, to impart wisdom and to guide the next generation of leaders on the right path. When you think back at your role models, what do you remember? And why? What is it about them, that you don't forget?

We remember the people who gave us a chance. This is undoubtedly something that could be beneficial to the development of Generation Z and their workforce.

All it takes is a manager or leader, giving them a chance, and investing in them to truly emerge as instrumental leaders, when they coach the younger generations, who will enter the workforce in the coming decades.

All the leadership styles we have mentioned, are probably the key ones for Generation Z. There are 11 different styles and not all are pertinent to our discussion of this group. You can go on any of our courses, to dive deeper into leadership and management styles.

However, the grounds for their more collaborative, democratic work approach stem from their background. Generation Z relies on these opportunities because they embody the values instilled in them since childhood. That fast-paced, common, diverse, and ever-changing environment will define their expectations, as well as the workforce we see as we age.

With this in mind, we must consider the influences on Generation Z that will shape their chosen leadership style. What we must also do is explain the distinction between management and leadership. There is always some uncertainty in this area, but Generation Z, the next generation of leaders, needs to comprehend these distinct principles.

There are different skill sets, and some people may make more natural leaders than managers. This is a topic for another day, but it is an important point nonetheless to bring up in our discussion on leadership and Generation Z.

The main area, and aim of this chapter is for you, as the reader, to think about Generation Z, and what their response will be to different leadership styles.

The key here is to understand and adapt our styles

accordingly to meet the needs, not just of the person, but also the generation we are working with.

We must also remember there is a certain standard to maintain, especially from a quality assurance perspective. There's also a style that needs to change depending on the situation, that needs to mirror this quality assurance expectation.

Still, that word once more that keeps appearing is communication, which is the important factor in determining whether or not a collaborative relationship between leaders, managers, and their staff is actually efficient.

In order to find out what works best for the individual, we need to communicate with them, ask them questions, to coach them, and investigate what works for them. On the other hand, there is no solution that is universally applicable and adapting is key.

For us, self-awareness is critical, and we must understand this ourselves. The EQ (Emotional Intelligence) part of being a leader is essential to get the absolute best from your team. Empathy is incredibly critical as a leader. And it's more than just a word.

There are plenty of social media platforms where you can discover all the necessary lingo, but how many people truly use it in their management?

It's always amusing to see someone quote this, but your instincts tell you it's insincere and someone else's words. If it is unnatural to go somewhere uncomfortable, you will avoid it.

This is something you notice when you are trained as a professional coach. When you watch the direction of travel and someone and watch what they are avoiding, you notice a fair bit about them as leaders and managers. It will be subtle, but it is still there.

You just have to pay attention.

In coaching, you can observe people directing a conversation to suit them, not the person they are coaching, mentoring, or training.

It's always an interesting observation and one we should focus on, because the majority of people don't actually realise they're doing this. They get lost in the mindset of "fix it, you're the mechanic!"

Whether you are leading Generation Z or managing them, you must take time to understand them, and comprehend how to integrate what they value in the organisation.

We understand that a lot of your working week may be taken up with this. Still, if you take the time and the early days to really understand these premises, your days will be much easier, as will your management and leadership in the organisation.

We feel it is vital at the start to spend time on this and keep the confusion as minimal as possible. The induction process is hugely important, so must be done well.

Motivation is a vast area, and we are not talking about the old Maslow's Hierarchy of Needs, even though it still stands. We have to think of what the science says. Science says AUTONOMY, MASTERY, AND PURPOSE are what drive us as individuals. As leaders or managers, it is important that we work with this theory because it absolutely works.

We should always be guided and aware of how we are making Generation Z feel. As mentioned before, people

will remember how you make
them feel but not what you say to them. That is why you remember the role models that made you feel a certain way, whether it be positive or negative, or a bit of both.

Every generation, but especially Generation Z, needs to concentrate on developing their intrinsic motivation in order to be successful in the job. Because members of Generation Z are becoming an increasingly significant element of the workforce in the present day, we need to pay attention and adjust.

We would like to bring to your attention the fact that there are five separate levels of leadership and management.

These levels are:

1. **The Highly Capable Individual:** This leader has talent, knowledge, skills, and exceptional work habits.

2. **The Contributing Team Member:** This leader makes contributions, and works effectively with others, to achieve collective goals.

. . .

3. The Competent Manager: This leader organises people, and resources, to meet goals, and facilitates the behind-the-scenes activities, necessary for success.

4. The Effective Leader: This leader moves their team toward a compelling vision, and stimulates high performance amongst their team members.

5. The Executive: This leader is simultaneously humble and professional and builds enduring greatness for the organisation.

As you can see, it's all about relationships. We keep saying this, but it is so true. It's the people who make the organisation, and all organisations have different kinds of relationships. This is where we must spend time to get the absolute best out of our individuals, and the team, because it's the people, who make any business a success.

Did you know that the majority of leaders only make it to the fourth level, and they struggle to make it to the fifth level with any success? The coaching conversations that we have had with board members have provided us with a lot of expertise in this area, which is where coaching comes in handy.

So, it's not just about Generation Z and the type of leadership they prefer, but about your leadership ability. Undoubtedly, adaptability and flexibility in yourself as a leader, are paramount to your success.

It's so crucial that you reflect on yourself and how you could do things differently, to help not only Generation Z, but other generations, even those within your demographic.

As we have discussed, there are so many skills that make good leadership, but there is one quality that is possibly the most challenging, and this is self-awareness.

Self-awareness requires you to focus on yourself. It's not the easiest thing to do, for somebody who is outwardly focused, as a leader.

Reflective journals can be a brilliant way to follow

your self-awareness. Ask yourself a few questions every day, notice how you act in different situations, and focus on how much listening you do.

Highlight moments where you realise how much you adapt and how much ownership you give in your question technique. These are just starting points, but important places to begin, if you want to cultivate self-awareness to become better as a leader.

Our Leader Journal available from Amazon

As a leader it would be wise, when dealing with Generation Z, to pay attention to these critical five areas:

1. Collaborate and Communicate

2. Allow for Independence and Autonomy
3. Implement Strategies for Work-Life Balance
4. Embrace New Technology
5. Emphasise Mental Health Needs

These areas, we have mentioned throughout this chapter, are incredibly important for Generation Z, and should be paramount in your leadership style, whatever it may be.

It is inevitable that different generations will face the same challenges that we have discussed with Generation Z. The percentages and the shift that we have observed with Generation Z, on the other hand, make it a much more significant problem.

We have only scratched the surface when it comes to leadership styles, but we hope that we have provided you with some food for thought in terms of how you can adapt, how you can change your perspective about Generation Z, and how we can all work together to pave a better path forward for our generations and the organisations that we continue to influence. There are a lot of things to think about when it comes to leadership styles.

If you would like to learn more about our management and leadership courses, which you can see on our website www.targettrg.co.uk

11

CORPORATE RESPONSIBILITY AND SUSTAINABILITY

In this chapter, we will explore corporate social responsibility and sustainability.

The first thing we must understand about Generation Z, is their keenness or approach, to sustainability. In our world today, sustainability has become an expected part of most—if not all—businesses, and

Generation Z recognises this and values the importance of this topic.

We believe they are very keen on a sustainable approach that could be seen as virtue signalling. It's about what they believe is the right decision, in terms of the planet, and maybe even in terms of what is societally acceptable.

Virtue signalling is often laughed at, as you may see in the press. We want to point out clearly, that we are not knocking them for virtue signalling. We believe it's just the mindset, that they believe when they feel passionately about something, then it is therefore, right.

From a passionate point of view, in terms of what they believe is the right way to be, Generation Z speaks a lot about sustainability. We think that they're quite influenced dramatically by social media, because they tend to believe most of what they read, even if it may not be accurate.

Let's take a second and review, as we discussed in our introduction, a bit about our background.

So, a part of our background that informs us as individuals, comes from many years ago when we were stationed in West Berlin as part of the Allied Force that was stationed there. We were positioned right behind the wall in 1986, almost 40 years ago. We used to laugh at the Germans when they had one waste bin for wet waste, one waste bin for dry waste, and another for hard waste. We used to laugh, when they were encouraged to wash their yoghurt cartons out, and so on.

When we were introduced to this, we asked, "What is this"? We were ignorant and uneducated about sustainability in those days, and now, we recognise how far the Germans were ahead of us, in terms of sustainability.

In older mindsets, there is some ignorance still and the belief that the sustainability doesn't matter, or that it's over discussed. Well, this is simply what we have heard and listened to in many of our training courses.

We believe that the young individuals of today's generations have a very different mindset, and that every little piece of effort when it comes to sustainability, counts in their perspective.

This can be a significant benefit to society, and we can all learn from this mindset, regardless of our generation, and of our belief or practice of sustainability, in our own lives currently.

However, we do believe that there is an element of persuasion on social media. Again, the opinion that they will have, Generation Z, is influenced by and large, by how much they live on social media, and it can even be driven further with the continued access and exposure to these topics. This is not a negative discussion by any means, because there are no doubt positive and negative effects, that come from this interaction.

Cynics will say that whoever is behind the social media platforms is definitely pushing an agenda. However, we do think that there's something there that is significantly important to discuss in terms of sustainability, something that we should all learn from, no matter where we are or how old we are.

AT THE END of the day, we want to be a part of a society in which we perform the appropriate actions, consistently safeguard both our earth and our people, and treat everyone with respect.

NOW, approaching this from the subject of managing them, how can they see a manager who's maybe a little bit older and still practising sustainability, in a way that is considered a little out of date?

You could generalise this because everybody is different, and there will be some managers who are totally on board, but there will also be some who are definitely not on board with the current expectations for sustainability today.

Generation Z will ultimately appreciate the manager who aligns with them, and their expectations of sustainability. More importantly, any company that has a more progressive outlook, which they believe is correct. Generation Z will always be guided by their values and principles, ensuring that their work consistently promotes benefits.

It is our belief that members of Generation Z will experience greater levels of happiness, if they are employed by businesses that demonstrate a commitment to sustainability, and that continue to demonstrate that they are working and performing particular duties, that encourage these efforts.

When it comes to attracting the attention of Generation Z, businesses who make environmentally friendly operations a priority, seek to lower their carbon footprint, and actively work towards environmental conservation will ultimately succeed.

This encompasses any, and all initiatives, to cut down on waste, give priority to renewable energy sources, and implement business practices that are environmentally responsible.

. . .

We think Generation Z is much happier in that environment, rather than an environment where sustainability appears to be ignored, or completely forgotten altogether. So, imagine a scenario now where we are working with someone in the Generation Z environment, and they work with us. There are clearly different ways that we see the world, and how we were brought up.

Let's face it: we may considerably disagree with each other, not only in how we view sustainability, but also in how we view specific values, expectations, and even the collaboration between team members.

In any event, you may find yourself in a situation where you simply say something innocuous over a cup of coffee or something similar, a simple throwaway comment that you take for granted. Even so, given their differing viewpoints on matters such as sustainability, how do you think they would react to this comment?

This is obviously an area where we need to be very careful about offending people without realising it. As they feel quite strongly about these areas, you know exactly what might happen, if you say something, that has the potential to be offensive. It is not uncommon that they may leave, when they are not happy with a company's values.

We know the values that they have are quite strong, as we keep mentioning throughout much of this book.

Generation Z is almost as guided by their values in much of what they do, not only professionally, but also in their personal lives. We've had plenty of discussions with them to know how important this issue is, and how much they prioritise this, over other areas. Simply put, other generations do not value their own principles above other matters as much as Generation Z does.

In situations where Generation Z feels their values have been betrayed, they may even go somewhere else, because the company isn't fully behind in terms of thinking and operating sustainability.

As Generation Z continues to become an even more significant part of today's workforce, and consumer markets, companies are forced to increase their adaptability, to meet these standards and to attract the majority of our consumer base today.

Because individuals change all the time, let's face it, a person only occupies a job role for a limited time, and with experience, you quickly learn that everyone is replaceable. Looking back 40 to 50 years, the picture in this region has changed dramatically between generations.

We believe that the days when you had a career for 20 years are long gone and different. Now, over the course of 20 years, people will likely have had about six different careers, which is far different from the reality that we grew up in, and what we were expecting in the workforce for our generation.

As we say, the values are quite strong, and there is no doubt if an organisation wants to keep someone, they have to seriously look at their values and the way that they think about such areas, including sustainability.

However, it's not just sustainability that is a critical area for Generation Z, it's also diversity. How does Generation Z see diversity compared to the way that we, as Baby Boomers, view it? We have a separate chapter later in this book, that discusses diversity, simply because, this is such a huge topic of concern, especially in regard to Generation Z.

Although older generations frequently discuss it; we believe Generation Z do not even notice diversity, as we do, because it is so new to us, as opposed to that of

Generation Z. They view diversity as an expected expectation in society, not just in the workplace. We now know that Generation Z does not even address this issue.

We have heard the following comments from them:

- *Why do you even mention this?*
- *Why do you even point this out?*

Simply put, it's people of our age group that are still talking about diversity. It was thrust onto us probably for a tick box exercise rather than clear education a few years ago.

THE MORE WE have learned over the last few years, the more we have seen such significant change. Let's face it, the pandemic has changed so many things, for so many individuals, both personally and professionally.

There are now organisations with such significantly different cultural perspectives, as the culture has changed so drastically, since a few years ago.

There are people from all around the world today within our organisations, and we need to respect each and every one of them, we need to respect what they bring to the table when we enter meetings and discuss monumental organisational projects and changes.

So it's pretty clear that we have gone through that transition, and now we always have to consider diversity. Let's be honest: we lived in a different world almost 20 to 30 years ago, and times have certainly changed. Just look back at the last 30 years. We remember ridiculous things, which were deemed illegal, where we worked.

It is true that we worked in a somewhat regimented setting that was controlled by white people and dominated by men. If diversity had been discussed in the past, it would have been ridiculed, and this is something that has changed for the better.

So, we know there are some people, leaders, and managers of a certain age, who may still carry some elements of this era. Many of them have not moved on, have not been educated, and are still sitting in that permanently fixed mindset.

What we mean, is that their perspectives may still be the same as they were back then, as they have not evolved with the changing environment, and values of today's world. Different sectors and organisations experience a vast variety of perspectives, but these areas of concern regarding diversity are still present.

We even have found that some people think that they have moved on, but when they engage in their training, it's pretty clear that some of them haven't. You can hear it in the language and the way that they talk about certain situations.

This is something that will be noticed by certain members of the Generation Z age group, but the change is still going on now. Because, as we have stated, Generation Z will soon constitute a significant portion of the labour force, it is imperative that we embrace them, learn from them, and continue to learn in order to pave the path for a more progressive future.

This can be a huge benefit here to genuinely embrace a more sustainable and diverse world, one that truly reflects the society and the leaders that are forming today. We will explore reverse mentorship in another chapter, and this can be a significant benefit here. One can never predict what will come after Generation Z. Everyone is free to speculate!

Interestingly enough, when we generalise now, Generation Z tends to be unable to cope with people who have an alternative opinion, or in other words, a diverse way of thinking. This is something else that we must consider in terms of managing them. Even then, research does show that because of social media pressure, and lack of critical thinking skills, people of this generation tend to bend.

. . .

LET us break this down further. What we mean is that when conflicts break out on social media, certain age groups will think in a specific way due to 'group think'. The younger age group will have quite different perspectives on whatever is being discussed in the discourse. Our point is that, while they are diverse and open to what we consider diversity, they are nevertheless closed in other ways.

We feel that again, this is due to a lack of critical thinking skills, social media and technology. This is what we call the Digital Triad.

What we have noticed is that if they think something different, they may want to speak out of turn. But because of the group mindset that they experience, they are more likely to clam up and not say anything. This can be individualised, but this is also a fact over all generations and age groups. But it is significantly different when we see it happening in Generation Z. This is a vast area that illustrates the challenges of facilitating these difficult conversations that everybody talks about needing to have.

It's not knowing how to have a critical conversation, or not knowing how to have a conversation when people's opinions are different, that's an issue. The ability to be able to communicate a difficult conversation with someone who has a different perspective, and agree to disagree, rather than trying to dissuade them, or persuade them of one perspective over the other.

We believe this is a development area for many in Generation Z and emotions are an issue here.

There is no doubt that we need to have an element of disagreement in every area of the workplace to move forward. Ultimately, leaders and managers will constantly be challenged, mainly if they go the wrong way about certain things like values and initiatives.

The best leaders and managers know this. If they are challenged and it is done in a practical way, then it's going to be a good thing for the entire company.

As professionals, we are aware that a challenge is beneficial, and that a disagreement that is constructive is what ultimately gives rise to progress. Because conflict may serve as a lever and a catalyst for transformative change, both in the workplace and within teams, it is essential for any business to have healthy conflict.

The problem is, if you stay silent, with a difference of opinion, then there will not be much movement forward. Generation Z does struggle with this, like all generations, but it's vastly different when we focus on this in our management training. It is crucial to understand as much as possible about how to help Generation Z in this area, not only to ensure smoother progress in companies, but to help them develop as leaders and managers.

Therefore, it is essential for organisations to have an understanding of how the values of different generations are communicated in relation to sustainability. If a company demonstrates responsibility in this area, it should be considered a significant achievement for Generation Z.

Another thing that we need to bear in mind is the fact that Generation Z is full of consumers that are conscientious about their purchasing decisions. It follows that individuals are more likely to choose to work for and purchase goods and services from businesses that exhibit ethical procedures, transparency, and a strong commitment to social and environmental responsibility.

Additionally, they are more likely to choose to work for such businesses.

Are you able to conceive of what this way of thinking would have been like around the 1980s? If we had done that back then, our lives would have been so drastically different, and we believe that this would have been a welcome change. For the time being, all we can do is view the advantages that come with Generation Z placing a significant emphasis on sustainability.

We need to encourage them to speak up and allow healthy conflict for us to all move forward and progress towards a healthier planet for all of us.

12

NAVIGATING FEEDBACK AND RECOGNITION IN THE WORKPLACE

In the workplace, feedback and acknowledgment are crucial for motivating employees, increasing productivity, and emphasising your team's performance. In this chapter, we will look at feedback and recognition, what good and negative feedback looks like, and other themes that are important in today's workplace and how to effectively manage them.

Together, we have over thirty years of experience in watching feedback be delivered and seeing how people receive this critical information.

Many of our roles entailed providing feedback—individually with a single employee or in a group. With endless hours of experience, we can speak to the good, the bad, and the forgotten aspects of feedback and recognition.

In any industry, feedback and recognition are essential because of the value that it provides. However, how does this differ when relating this topic to Generation Z? That's a question we will answer in this chapter. But first, let's dive deep into the differences between good, and bad feedback, including the traps and catch-out areas that you should be mindful of.

Given our experience, it is easy for us to pick out what good and bad feedback looks like. Good feedback accomplishes a few important goals. First, it's sincere. You share genuine insights with your employees or team members, but you also do so, in a way that matches how they prefer to be recognised. If your employee is generally shy and reserved, the best protocol is likely to deliver this feedback in private, rather than in front of other team members.

Furthermore, good feedback is also frequent and personalised. To have an impact with feedback, you must share it more often and let your employees know what they are doing is working. That means not just recognising the awards, but the effort they put in every day. On the other hand, lousy feedback is easy to spot.

Poor feedback may be given infrequently, and it may sound generic and insincere, leaving your employees wondering how they are performing because they believe what you said was repeated to others around them. Understanding these distinctions, traps, and catch-out regions, among other indicators of bad or good feedback, can help you enhance your management abilities. More significantly, it will teach you how to communicate with the diverse members of your crew.

What we know about feedback, from our decades of experience, is that there is a right and wrong way to deliver it and that feedback is crucial. We cover this with multiple generations in our management training and the importance of meeting different generations with specific ways of communicating this feedback.

Feedback models work well, but these are frameworks that you can utilise to deliver this pertinent information. This brings us to how you can improve your staff member's reception of feedback. It begins with two words: growth mindset.

You must be aware of two kinds of mindsets: a fixed mindset and a growth mindset. Fixed mindsets are individuals who believe that their skills are crystallised and that change is not easy. On the other hand, those with growth mindsets believe they are adaptable, capable of change, and can

use feedback to their advantage.

Can you guess which type of person is more receptive to feedback?

You guessed right: growth mindsets are typically more receptive to feedback, while those with fixed mindsets struggle. They find themselves wanting to avoid the input and the comments that they might receive. To them, any negative feedback is something immovable and unchangeable.

However, we may encourage them to view things differently. By creating development mindsets and encouraging individuals to seek feedback, we may gradually—but effectively—allow people to adjust to the expectation of receiving this feedback from their supervisors.

When you consistently encourage your team members to seek feedback and to embrace this without fear, they will begin to see this as an opportunity to learn. That's when the real power is seen. They can take your feedback and implement the changes, and soon, you'll start to see shifts in the workplace and further development of each employee.

The more people embrace a growth mindset, the less fearful feedback can be, and the more impactful it will become to the people willing to see the value of what you provide for them. Each dose of feedback will be the morsels of wisdom they use as opportunities to learn from their mistakes, making them even more prepared, engaged employees at your organisation.

Now that you understand how to prepare people to receive this feedback and recognition, let's examine how to deliver feedback. Feedback can be short or formal. For some people, they like to utilise FAST FEEDBACK. This FAST FEEDBACK is short, sweet, and to the point, which makes everyone feel at ease when preparing for management's comments. You can also deliver more FORMAL FEEDBACK. This can be in the form of regular employee performance assessments or a report. that offers tangible, accurate information for your workers to view and evaluate.

Regardless of how you deliver your feedback, it should have a balance of positives and areas of improvement. Some may even call this a compliment sandwich; we call it the bathtub and it is much more than a sandwich! We are not going to go into detail in this chapter and it is something we cover in detail on our management courses.

You can provide a positive, some areas of improvement, and then close on other positive notes that you need to share with your employees.

If you follow this format, not only will you empower

your employees, but you will see great results. You may want to skip the format and deliver feedback, but trust us—how you deliver your feedback has vastly different results. If you put yourself in your colleague's shoes, you can make effective choices about how you provide feedback, in what format, and to what extent to have the best results.

One common problem that we have seen in the industry these days is the challenge of rushed feedback. People can deliver feedback quickly, but rushed feedback has its challenges. Managers will hurry to provide the input, rather than taking the time to go through the points, explaining why this feedback is being delivered in such a manner, and then wait for questions. Arguably, this is one of the most critical challenges when it comes to management, especially in managing the Generation Z workers in your company.

Even if pressed for time, we must consider how Generation Z feels about this feedback and their preference. Personalising the feedback has excellent results, and can encourage people to take the commentary to heart, as they implement it into their work. Delivering rushed feedback, especially for Generation Z, is different from how to gather their trust. You should take the time to explain the comments, ensure that they understand what you have presented, and also, have time to ask any questions they may have.

Another common issue we have seen as professionals is the need for feedback to be more objective. Feedback can be objective. However, it should also be tasked focus. It will provide much more benefit to your employees, if you can explain the specific tasks they need to improve rather than remaining too objective. For example, suppose a major project has just been completed on your marketing team. In that case, you can deliver specific feedback about the tasks completed to ensure that future work meets or exceeds expectations. Delivering generic feedback should be avoided, not just because it needs more value, but because it is also limited in its actionability.

Remaining too objective—like rushing feedback—also tends to come off as cold and calculated. Even if you work in an industry where complex numbers are the expectation, you shouldn't approach your feedback similarly. Focus on incorporating positives wherever you can, especially with your Generation Z workers. You will gain their trust if you do this, as they value positive, warm, and encouraging comments, rather than cold, calculated, and rushed content; that leaves them wondering where they stand as workers in your organisation.

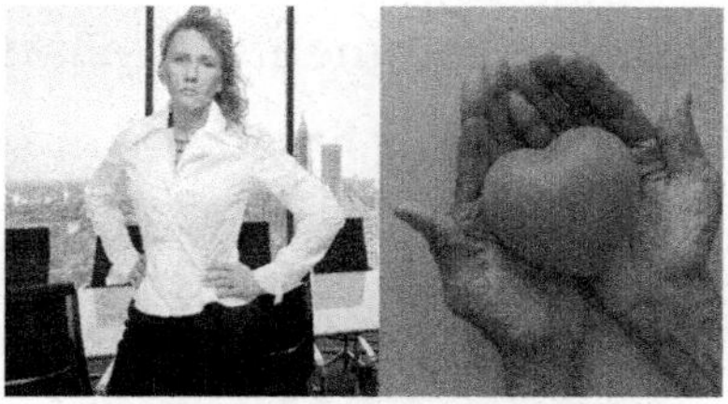

Arguably, there is a way to deliver short feedback and still be valuable; rather than giving rushed feedback, a simple "Great work today because..." can provide great value for your employees. However, we have seen the more formal approach to feedback—through tools, effective question technique, and other factors—succeed more in establishing rapport and handling relationships masterfully.

To build the relationships you need with your Generation Z employees, emphasise FORMAL FEEDBACK, but feel free to use SHORT FEEDBACK when appropriate, and after rapport has been established.

REGARDLESS OF HOW you deliver feedback, it will only matter how compelling your comments are, if Generation Z is encouraged to take your feedback positively. One of the main reasons that Generation Z, as compared to other generations, struggles to take feedback, is because many of them were raised with an abundance of positive feedback.

When they receive commentary that may be seen as critical, even if posed as an area for improvement, they struggle to see it positively. It makes sense: if you heard all of your life that you were terrific and you could do everything you set your mind to, wouldn't you struggle with criticisms and suggestions for improvement?

When people around the world have raised their kids in cultures where everyone is equal, it can be hard to recognise differences, especially areas of improvement that require attention to work on.

It hurts to learn that we will not all be the best footballers in the country, and arguably, this might be one failure of today's society. Regardless of this societal issue, we can all do our part to encourage Generation Z not to fear feedback, but to embrace it positively, and see its value.

We must encourage our workers, especially Generation Z, as many say that today's generations are not as strong as they once were. All around the world—even in different cultures—we find there is a significant challenge of Generation Z being perceived as a weaker generation.

As managers, we have an opportunity to empower our Generation Z workers, and guide them, to become strong leaders so that they too, can elevate the next generation of workers, to see value in the feedback, and recognition they receive in the workplace.

That's why it is essential to focus on the emotional resiliency of our Generation Z workers. We must empower them to think positively, dream bigger, and see the value in continuous improvement through feedback. In all actuality, this should apply to every generation in the workplace today. We all could benefit from more emotional resiliency!

Let's face it: we all think that we have to protect our kids—even over-protect, in our opinion—and this likely has roots in how the Baby Boomers didn't have anything. We want to provide for our kids and give them all we never had. We have seen it in many families in our home country and worldwide.

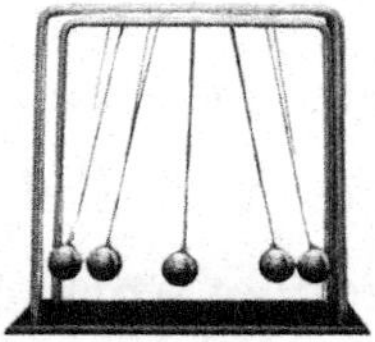

We liken this situation to a pendulum, and how they swing. Several years ago, adversity was dealt with, but not now, the pendulum has swung the other way. We believe it has gone too far, in our minds, it is time to make it more balanced, as it is not only what is best for the future, but it is our job as the older generation.

Older generations are tasked with preparing the next generation to lead the future to a prosperous age. We guide and bring people to the future, providing them not only with the learning that we have cultivated, but also with the insights that we have found that need to be refined and theorised. We learn from our mistakes to teach the younger generations, empowering and educating them and making them more robust in the workplace and life.

When we hear comments about how people need to bounce back, this gets us thinking about one area: coaching. This phrase, "bounce back," is a common phrase used to get others to toughen up, but what does it mean? Additionally, to what level does someone need to “bounce back”? Furthermore, “bounce back” from what?

As we think about how we raise our kids today, we're in charge of decision-making, as our kids are with us as parents for longer. Back in our generation and the Baby Boomer generation, there were no cars. We walked everywhere, left school at sixteen, and always had a Saturday job. We always had plenty of work available, so we never worried about getting a job. Best of all, there were no university fees. But only 3% of the population went to university. Arguably, things have dramatically changed, leading to the fact that Generation Z needs us more, than we needed our parents.

Generation Z needs their parents longer at no fault of their own. Simple as that! Society has placed them where we all must adapt and support them. The generations before us were working at fourteen, so there continues to be a constant transition. There is no right way to proceed, but the main focus should be adaptation as we continue to empower and support Generation Z, in finding their success and resiliency.

It is not just the responsibility of the parents, but also of the organisations to teach the importance of receiving balanced feedback. In order to assure growth, we need to teach how to provide constructive comments. As a result of the fact that a large number of individuals have to be made aware of the necessity of knowing how they have performed, feedback is rarely provided.

In the event that you are a manager, and find yourself thinking in this manner, you run the risk of falling into the trap of not providing sufficient feedback, since you want feedback for yourself less.

It's critical to give feedback, because of the generational challenges and to say it correctly. Delivery goes a long way but also guarantees to motivate your team members. Even just a few positive words can impact people so much. So, if you are a manager uncomfortable with feedback, it's about something other than you. Feedback is about the other person, so you must get used to delivering feedback to support and motivate others.

Feedback is not just a tool, but so much more than that. Adapting it to Generation Z, we must meet them where they are: with short, quick, positive feedback that gets to the point. Encouraging them to ask for feedback is enough, but how would they like to receive it?

Unlike other generations, social media plays an integral part in this effort. It might be interesting to ask our Generation Z counterparts if they prefer email, WhatsApp, face-to-face, or written feedback. The truth is, it is probably different for everyone. But there's no harm in asking to meet people, where and how, they want their feedback delivered.

This is also an important question to ask in the face of conflicts. Why not ask if they prefer confronting the issue head-on, or remotely, if they struggle with these difficult conversations?

We imagine the answers will be a mixed bag. Even if you ask every age group, it will be even more diverse in scope.

The bottom line is to improve our communication skills, especially regarding feedback and recognition. If you gathered any crucial findings from this chapter, let it be that communication remains critical in the workplace, and when dealing with conflicts. If nothing else, the more we communicate, the more we understand one another.

Returning to feedback and recognition, regardless of how Generation Z desires this commentary, formal reports can be annual appraisals or six-month reviews, dependent on how your organisation wants to perform this.

On the other hand, informal feedback can be a short few sentences—even a few words—that can go a long way. The common area that is missed—that should be emphasised regardless—is the "why". Don't forget to tell your team members why you said what you said.

If someone struggles with feedback in your workplace, let this be a sign, that they may struggle with encouragement. This could be the opportunity where you step up, to bridge the gap, to encourage them to see this as a positive, not a negative. It could be up to you to flip their perspective.

THE MOST IMPORTANT rule of thumb is to follow your instinct. If your instinct tells you to do something, follow it and use it when it comes. A coaching technique that takes much time to teach, and learn, is listening to your instincts.

If you listen to your gut, you can become a better communicator. Furthermore, remember your values. This can help you stay aligned both individually and within your organisation. Don't just treat this as a checklist; see the value in aligning your actions with your values and your feedback with it all the same.

AS WE CLOSE THIS CHAPTER, there is always the opportunity to change your style regarding feedback and recognition. The use of digital platforms can become unparalleled in your workplace. Why not change your style to meet the needs of your Generation Z team members?

The older generations will need to get used to it, but with so many AI tools appearing, who knows how long it will be, before we all use these feedback methods?

The bottom line is that if you are positive, Generation Z will follow suit due to your leadership. Your teamwork and collaboration are vital for them, because of their vastly different experiences, and their need for encouragement.

It is necessary for them to be in an atmosphere that is both open and optimistic. There are a great number of impressive companies that have been at the forefront of change by adjusting their settings to accommodate the growing number of Generation Z employees. They are providing possibilities for progress, and personal growth, that are of the utmost importance.

It is essential to keep in mind that the manner in which we carry out all of these activities is also of the utmost significance. The empowerment of a generation of leaders who will continue to have the same beneficial influence, will be achieved, if we continue to provide Generation Z, with assistance through the provision of constructive criticism and recognition.

13

THE POWER OF MENTORSHIP AND REVERSE MENTORING

In this chapter, we aim to look at mentoring and reverse mentoring, including exploring the differences between mentoring, and coaching, as well as how this can impact Generation Z.

We start this chapter, by first looking at what mentoring is, as there is some confusion about the differences between mentoring and coaching. Many people we have found often mix them up, but these are two distinct concepts.

So, mentorship is defined as:

> 'The relationship in which a more experienced and more knowledgeable person helps to guide a less experienced or less knowledgeable person. It is a learning, and development partnership between someone with vast experience, and someone who wants to learn.'

On the other hand, coaching is distinctly different. Coaching is defined as:

> 'A conversation between the coach and coachee, whereby the coachee, achieves a higher level in understanding of awareness, and self-awareness, whilst the coach provides the safe environment, and structure for the outcome to occur.'

As you can see, these two terms are different. While coaching is a significant aspect of organisations, leadership, and more, we will look at mentorship, not coaching, in this chapter.

With mentoring, you know you have to have the skill set required, which is critical to being a mentor for somebody else. You also need to have the experience, understand what the job entails, and fully understand what your mentee is looking for.

Don't worry if you have questions at this stage, because we will look at reverse mentoring later in this chapter, answering any questions you may have about mentorship and how you can become a better mentor.

So, suppose you're a manager, and have identified mentors for young individuals in your organisation. In that case, you first need to educate the mentors, which is absolutely crucial, if you want to see success with a mentorship program.

THIS CREATES the foundation for an excellent mentor-mentee connection. This initial step is critical because everyone understands that it is relationships that build individuals, who then develop the organisation. Without effective mentorship facilitation, and without genuine involvement or growth from the younger members of your firm, you may find yourself with undeveloped talent that impedes your capacity to succeed.

We think that every organisation is in development.

We need to realise how unique each organisation is. We do not want everyone or every organisation to be the same. Recognising each individual's distinct skill sets is critical to fostering a varied and successful workplace, particularly given today's generational demographics.

We must be extremely careful not to stigmatise Generation Z, especially given some of the distinctions we have identified. We're all different. We must remember that we have all been conditioned to behave in a specific way, which is precisely what this conversation is about. That is precisely what mentorship is all about: recognising how we have been conditioned to behave, and how we can assist younger generations, in capitalising on their strengths while improving on their faults.

When it comes to the mentor and mentee relationship, the mentee should be able to choose their mentor, and not just be given one because the ownership of this mentorship relationship from both parties involved is absolutely crucial. It can also go extremely wrong if the mentor takes on a mentee, with no pre-meeting and understanding of how they can help each other. This is what we term a 'chemistry call.'

A 'chemistry call' can be the key to development, because, without chemistry between individuals in a relationship, it can be difficult to truly facilitate any growth or development. This is absolutely vital in coaching, so it should be exactly the same for mentorship.

The relationship is the most important aspect of a successful mentorship experience, so if the mentee believes they have found the proper person, they have.

Even with the most experienced mentor, having the wrong relationship can hinder the development of the younger mentee. Nothing happens with bad relationships, so we must focus on facilitating better relationships, and connections, between the mentor and the mentee before the mentorship begins.

This is not what you are looking for!

Let us now go on to the training. The mentor must have a training package in place, as well as a standardisation and quality assurance programme. This is definitely necessary since mentorship should include training that is beneficial to the younger mentee.

The mentor must understand young people, particularly Generation Z. They must not only have the necessary skills and experience to provide value to younger generations, but they must also comprehend Generation Z. We've already covered a lot of it in this book, so the understanding is already there, but it's vital to learn from these lessons.

But then, it's not just the mentor that has to do the work to understand the mentee, as Generation Z also needs to understand other generational groups, and even their own mentor. It's all about education for both sides involved.

As a mentor, you must understand how to motivate and deliver effective feedback, both formally and informally. We discussed the basics of this earlier in the book. Generation Z loves goal setting, also discussed in this book. They are very used to setting goals through the education system, which they expect, even in the professional realm.

They also enjoy being recognised, which may go a long way when exhibited. As you may have noticed, the older generations struggle with this, since they are task-oriented, and have not been trained or conditioned, to give out thanks as readily.

These mentors must take accountability, thus their questioning approach must be effective in order to pull everything from the mentee. Along with questions, the ability to understand, and listen is also important. The mentor must respect the other person by actually hearing what they say, waiting to respond, and seeking understanding first.

As we always suggest to our mentor trainees, the focus should be on questioning rather than telling. We can't emphasise enough the importance of this key skill set.

ONE FANTASTIC METHOD is to keep a journal of your questioning and listening techniques. This will allow you to focus more on them. Believe it or not, mastering this skill can take a long time, and asking the incorrect question, at the wrong moment might, cause a huge breach in your relationship.

The more you focus on the quality and timeliness of your questions, the better your relationship with your mentee will be as a mentor. If you are truly committed, all it takes is 5 minutes a day this helps the focus on these crucial areas.

Many people may boast about their listening abilities, but unless trained, they will not truly comprehend them at various levels, even if they have read and studied them themselves. We know this from our training courses, since everyone tells you everything about it. Still, they have no concept how to put them into practice in the real world.

The truth is that we don't listen well enough! We'd like to believe that we listen as much as we tell others, but we can all improve our listening abilities. A difficult skill to learn.

As a result, we feel mentors require monitoring, as we cannot enable them to guide without evaluating their skills and impact. Both sides must be checked from a quality assurance perspective. A truly effective mentorship programme is extremely difficult to implement without a thorough grasp of the importance of assurance in this process.

We must consider how mentorship has developed and grown, while also remembering, that it occurred spontaneously years ago. Passing through a corridor and making a cup of coffee were minor discussions, but this was how mentoring was done back then.

These little moments of simply asking someone a question were essential, but have been drastically curtailed as a result of the transition between working from home and the office. Those interactions proved beneficial over time, highlighting the importance of mentorship in our lives. Nonetheless, we must pay a greater emphasis now due to our world's new hybrid nature.

Since the pandemic, all you have is meetings after meetings, and it's not the same. It makes no difference if the meeting is held on Teams or Zoom. We've been in workplaces where they put up virtual 10-minute coffee breaks, which is still better than nothing. Still, it is not the same as being in the same room with someone and being able to ask them questions without time constraints or technical obstacles.

We believe that mentoring has gained in popularity, particularly among Baby Boomers and Millennials. Many people are recognising the value of mentorship and highlighting the importance of seeking it out, even outside of the job. We've put up a few mentorship programmes in recent years; let's be honest, this would not have been a course years ago.

In addition to this, we believe it's also critical to ask the mentee how they would like to be mentored, which is a great way to start their relationship. Why not ask them exactly what they need, and how they can best benefit from mentorship?

We have found that even talking to them about social media, what works and what doesn't, is an effective way to begin understanding how to communicate, and truly impact these younger generations.

. . .

USE THE BASIC COACHING ANALOGY –

> If you are standing on one side of the river, and need to get to the other side, what do you need to get there?

From there, we can work on a program together; we suggest structure and communication. Communication is a massive aspect of this, as we have touched on this in the book. Your communication must be effective, and we have provided several different ways to effectively communicate with Generation Z.

Training for these areas is huge, so you must complete these, to help the mentor, and the mentee experience a better relationship through mentorship.

However, we must impress again that training is so different from mentorship. Training is best defined as:

> 'Training is teaching, or developing in oneself or others, any skills and knowledge that relate to the specific useful competencies. Training has specific goals for improving one's capability, capacity, productivity, performance, maintaining, upgrading, and updating skills throughout working life.'

When we realise that training is different, we must be careful not to mix them up, and it is critical that you understand your position at all times. Whether you're the mentee or the mentor, this all counts, and the training varies.

UNDERSTANDING what role the mentor and mentee have and their relationships is critical. Both of these individuals need to understand relationships, and people, especially those who differ from themselves.

We know this is a huge area, so we cover this in our management courses, so every leader and manager is fully informed, of all they need to know about improving, and creating better relationships in the workplace.

It is really important to understand how you come across, because, how you think you come across, may not necessarily be so.

We already know that Generation Z will be ahead of us in a biased world, more so than Baby Boomers and Millennials. They have lived and breathed it for years, so the other generations can learn from them. This is a critical area for reverse mentoring.

HOWEVER, we believe that mentor is not just a word, but so much more than that. Mentor is a role that holds so much importance beyond what words can express. However, let's get to the next topic, what do we mean by reverse mentoring?

THE OBVIOUS RESPONSE is the antithesis of what we have already written! Number one, this is a wonderful incentive for Generation Z, allowing them to mentor and have a real impact on others. Remember, Generation Z wants nothing more than to change the world, so what better way to do so than through reverse mentorship?

Generation Z will be super sharp regarding information technology, and digital tools. They have a great amount of knowledge to use in the digital area, that can help other generations.

We think it's ridiculous not to use them and harness their skill sets, but some people haven't received the message, and there's no structured mentorship to allow Generation Z to teach us more about digital tools and technology.

As Baby Boomers, we have had IT issues of our own, and we have frequently sought assistance from our son with various tools. Despite the fact that we believe we are doing well, we are not! In light of this, we are of the opinion that it is an important and beneficial mentorship field for Generation Z to teach others who are older, what they know. We only hope they have more patience than our son!

We must remember that Generation Z has been exposed to the digital world since they were five years old. As we write this, we see children even younger, which sparks a new conversation about how they will behave in the workplace and what digital technology they will be more proficient with.

With all this in mind, how do you think Generation Z will feel about the ownership and responsibility of teaching technology skills? Fantastic is what we would say because they will embrace this opportunity, ownership is so important. Some organisations have twigged to this, but are among the minority today.

Generation Z will be intrinsically motivated, and buy into the mentoring practice immediately, if offered. There may be problems with persuading older generations, especially those with a more fixed mindset, because they think they may not benefit from generational reverse mentorship, especially with Generation Z. However, like other issues we discussed, we believe this will be a minority issue.

Sadly, there will always be a few egos and some

huge body armour around, especially older generations. When it comes to showing that they don't know something, because showing any vulnerability, could be an issue for them. We believe that a mindset shift is needed here, because we speak a lot on this topic, and see how people experience these issues regularly in coaching.

Remember, as discussed in other sections, it could be an issue with dysfunctional teams. If we don't express our vulnerabilities, then we never truly build the trust needed, especially the trust required for leadership, and efficiency in the workplace.

What we must do is allow Generation Z to reach out to other generations. They must teach older generations, and the latter must accept the new technological skill sets accessible to them. If your organisations leaders have not already done so, we believe senior management should become involved in promoting this.

JUST PICTURE how fantastic reverse mentoring is! As we have seen, it works, so why wouldn't you do this for your organisation?

Some key areas that are required for mentoring, and reverse mentorship, are likely to be in goal setting. We have mentioned that Generation Z will be used to this, because it's not an alien language to them.

There will likely be confusion without goals set ahead of time! They will use these goals to set expectations, and to see progress, as they are likely very ambitious, because of this expected learned behaviour with goal setting.

Critical thinking and adaptability are other key areas we believe will be critical for mentorship. It has been recognised that Generation Z needs mentoring and training in this area. Being more flexible, is critical for any organisation, so any opportunity to bring this into the mentoring package is extremely helpful.

Generation Z also enjoys having assistants in the modern workplace, with ideas on navigating and professional networking, including personal development. With personal development, we highly recommend focusing on areas like SELF-IMPROVEMENT, SELF-REFLECTION, and even JOURNALING, as they enjoy the process, and it isn't new to them.

Emotional intelligence, remember EQ, is another critical factor here and the future of management is emotional intelligence. Aside from EQ, work-life balance is another issue we have mentioned in this book, as is the importance of building resilience.

Generation Z can benefit significantly from what we

can teach them, especially in becoming resilient, they are the new leaders for the upcoming decades.

As you can tell, there are so many areas to consider, but it's about prioritisation. We have spoken to many human resources and leadership and development leads. Many believe, these areas are great learning opportunities for mentoring programs for Generation Z.

Remember: there is no one-size-fits-all. We have to remember that Generation Z may be fragmented, due to the constant digital stimuli, so we must be able to tailor our mentorship, and diverse mentorship opportunities appropriately, to ensure everybody receives the benefits. So, with that, our advice is to keep mentoring sessions dynamic, short, and interactive.

WE HOPE this chapter has given you a lot to think about and some important insights on mentoring for Generation Z.

But there is so much value that the older generations can provide in regards to resilience, emotional intelligence, and even personal development; there's so much to learn and so much to facilitate.

However, we can't forget the importance of reverse mentorship, especially in terms of the digital tools and technologies that Generation Z is proficient in, and from, which we can all learn.

With these insights, your organisation can implement similar mentorship, and reverse mentorship opportunities, to significantly impact your efficiency and your employees.

14

GENERATION Z AND PERSONAL DEVELOPMENT

Personal development is one of the critical areas that we have found necessary for Generation Z. This is a distinct characteristic of this unique generation.

In this chapter, we will dive deep into Generation Z and their views on personal development, why this matters, how managers and leaders can encourage this in the workplace, and what it can do for our Generation Z employees.

We believe that a chapter on this topic would be fascinating and valuable for almost any manager, leader, or organisation. Particularly, those focused on enhancing and adopting greater professional development.

ANY BUSINESS LEADER should be aware that personal development possibilities are more important to Generation Z than remuneration, and company status. Generation Z places a high importance on personal development, which has been one of the most noticeable characteristics in our coaching, and training sessions with this group.

When it comes to hiring, developing, and maintaining Generation Z talent, there is little question that organisations need to make learning, and development programmes, a key component of their strategies. It is important to keep in mind that they are gradually becoming a larger percentage of the workforce. The fact that they are gaining control is, of course, very logical, considering that we were once the dominant workforce, and once we seized control ourselves!

Without doubt, Generation Z generally has a very

proactive approach, as they continually seek opportunities to learn and grow. This is quite unique compared to other generations, especially considering what studies have confirmed regarding the significance of personal development to this generation. Orbi, a Swedish company based in Gothenburg, researched personal development, and found out how important personal development truly was, for Generation Z.

OVER THE COURSE of many years, a great deal of study has been conducted in this field, and the findings are, for the most part, unequivocal. In first place, according to the findings of the research that was published, 14.1% of the total replies from the study revealed that personal growth was the most essential factor.

The fact that personal development received almost ten times more interactions than other areas, such as additional holiday weeks, and even more than twice as many as salary development, demonstrates, in our opinion, a clear distinction between the values and priorities of this generation. This is because personal development is such an important benefit to Generation Z.

There is no doubt that Generation Z will be highly different from all the generations before them. Not everyone will say that personal development takes higher precedence in the workplace, especially over more time off for holidays and even more pay. For older generations, we know that there will probably be a different prioritisation. A different balance, so to speak, of what truly matters when seeking out work with a particular company.

Some of the other facts from research that has been uncovered on personal development, and Generation Z, have read very much the same; pointing to even more unique differences in this generation as compared to older ones, even ours.

The second most important issue for Generation Z —with 13.9% of all responses classified as such—is the necessity for remote job opportunities. This well-received bonus illustrates that Generation Z believes that hybrid work is essential, particularly in light of the pandemic, and the changes that many businesses had to make, in order to continue operations.

Understandably, Generation Z wanted to maintain a work-life balance and avoid having to return to work five days a week, face to face, because they didn't see the need in being in the workplace if more work could be done from the comfort of their own home.

There are other arguments from different age groups, sectors, and even the public or commercial sectors, but this is Generation Z's perspective, and it explains why they believe hybrid work is an absolute must in the future, and a priority for them, as they seek employment. The viewpoints on this area are all extremely different. They contrast significantly. But when it comes to Generation Z, this is a pretty big area for them and a clear difference between other generations.

Surprisingly, in sixth place in this survey, Generation Z prioritises competitive pay as well. However, it received half as many interactions on the poll as personal development, indicating that this is not as important to Generation Z, as it was to previous generations. This feels unexpectedly low for Baby Boomers and Millennials, but it's clear, that Generation Z prioritises hybrid work, and personal development over this.

AS EXPECTED, the older generations will value pay higher on the scale of priorities, but probably not behind personal development. However, every person is different, so each priority scale will likely look different depending on who you talk to. Nevertheless, you're hopefully starting to understand why organisations may need to think differently, and the mindset that we must take, to see a pathway for the future to effectively support Generation Z. Some key businesses have already grasped this, and will be working closely with

Generation Z. Still, we believe that more companies need to do the same.

Companies cannot ignore older generations, however, because they must collaborate closely with them, to build what suits them, and their ideal work environment. These priorities may be more important than the majority.

We believe that some businesses and managers are far more adaptable between generations, in terms of opportunities, and rewards, which might be quite beneficial.

We feel that it's essential to mention what came up later in the study which adds relevance: bonus systems.

The topic of a bonus system, and its perceived benefit, is absolutely significant. We have covered this area so many times in our management courses and from various angles. One thing to recognise is that a bonus system alone, is not a motivating factor, especially compared to what many people believe about bonus systems. A bonus system can work appropriately with other appropriate motivators, but it should never be solely relied upon to motivate employees.

Despite these findings, it's important to state that the research may have targeted different age groups, and those who have just left university. Hence, it's challenging to imagine yourselves on a level for a bonus, which is likely why these were lower on the priority list.

However, we also feel it's important to highlight the fifteenth position: healthcare insurance. This fascinating finding has a few explanations as to why it was in this position, and most of it comes down to geographical differences, and cultural expectations for employment.

Now, this can be viewed differently, depending on whether your country has public health care or not. In countries like the United Kingdom, we have a public health care system. Thus, we must consider the age that this will come a factor.

Being over 40 years old, you think more about health than you do at the age of 20, so age brings different thoughts and feelings regarding health insurance, as well as different priorities and considerations for one's personal health.

Regardless of what research you read, and what country you reside in, you will find that Generation Z places significant importance on personal development, as the key motivator, in the organisation they aspire to work for.

In summary, Generation Z prioritises opportunities to learn, and grow, as the top driver of work culture. This will likely change the way that managers, leaders, and their organisations attract and retain talent.

Generation Z sees that by focusing on communication skills, continuous learning, admitting ignorance, seeking mentorship, embracing the advantage, fostering innovation, creative thinking, practising reflection and goal setting, they can thrive. This will likely set a unique precedent moving forward, for future generations that come into the workplace, in tomorrow's highly digital culture.

As we have discussed in this book, Generation Z is well used to goal setting. This process is a unique part of their education system, and something that they were brought up with. To the point that they feel it's bizarre to not have goals, which makes it even easier for them to prioritise personal development, based on this expectation.

Of course, goal setting was never thought about years ago because we're talking about the 1970s and 1980s. Yet, it has become a bit of a thing today. So many people talk about it, but Generation Z is so much more used to it, than any other generation that we have encountered.

As mentioned before, let's not forget about Generation Z and their prioritisation of a work-life balance, because they see personal and professional development, as distinctly interconnected. They will seek opportunities that align with their values and interests, viewing personal growth, not just as a means to advance their career, but also to lead a fulfilling life, both personally and professionally.

There is a high probability that members of Generation Z will have more than one career, a greater number of positions, and employment than any other elder generation can ever remember having.

All of this is something that needs to be taken into consideration by us when we are handling Generation Z. The importance of personal growth is something that we strongly believe should be emphasised in mentoring and coaching programmes.

In the event that your organisation has not yet acknowledged the differences that Generation Z possesses, in terms of their entrepreneurial spirit, it is important to keep in mind that this generation places a high value on taking the initiative, and being self-reliant. As a consequence, they will actively seek out possibilities for their own personal and professional development.

With such easy access to information on the Internet, and online platforms, Generation Z is accustomed to seeking out knowledge independently, without any direction or motivation from others.

This may influence their approach to personal development, because, they are much more likely to take the initiative, in finding the resources, and opportunities for learning themselves, even if not presented initially. So, if the opportunities are not there, then they may leave.

Think of the money that it costs to bring someone in, and then they walk away after a short duration with the company. Once they realise the opportunities are not there, we all know that the cost of recruiting can be, exorbitantly high, much like throwing money away!

MANY GENERATIONS WILL EXPRESS a desire for their work to have a meaningful impact on society. Personal development is not just a means to advance professionally, but also a way to contribute positively to the world. We've previously mentioned that Generation Z will, in their lifetime, run a business on the side, as this is not unusual for them. Their access and understanding of the Internet allow this naturally, giving them the opportunity to explore passions, and side projects that they see value in.

Generation Z will also often engage in informal learning through online courses, tutorials, and other non-traditional avenues. They are far more likely and inclined to explore a variety of learning resources, beyond traditional educational methods and institutions.

This is so different from the world that we grew up

in, especially in how well-informed they are to our era, indicating a pretty massive difference, in the accessible education and the pursuit of such.

Their global perspective may influence a lot of their personal development goals, as they have an emphasis on understanding diverse perspectives and fostering a global mindset.

WHAT IS essential for anyone to reflect on is that this is a trend, and individuals have attitudes towards personal development, and continued professional development that will vary widely. Even despite the generation they may belong to, plus, as Generation Z ages and grows in the workplace, this emphasis on personal development may change, and their perspectives, as expected, may evolve even further.

One thing we do have, is a lot of expertise, and we've observed that Generation Z benefits greatly from our training. We believe it is because they are so used to working online or being lectured. Although a training course can be intimidating at first, they quickly adapt, engage, and end up loving it.

Only a few months ago, a group of 10 were completely out of their comfort zone during one of our sessions. They were used to online education, or boring PowerPoint facilitation. Initially, they sat uncomfortably, but we drew them in slowly, just to keep them as comfortable as possible and to nudge them outside of their comfort zones. We encouraged them to engage, and interact, to truly become a part of the learning process.

They were all managers, which was really alarming. Consider for a moment or two the pressure they were under, and the expectations that had been placed on them.

Ultimately, they took so much from the training, and everyone said they had never had anything like this, which shocked us. We reflected a lot on this experience from our side and our expectations. It became evident to us that the difference between the generations, is primarily in how they receive training, and their expectations of such.

Things had to change, and we took advantage of the opportunity that the pandemic presented. The epidemic enabled us to create our digital platforms, but we mostly utilise them as a supplement to our courses, with monthly coaching calls for groups to implement the knowledge.

We do not believe that any learning that is done just online works, based on our experience, as we have watched and participated in such instances. For us, this educational experience is minimal. It wastes money, and is not too great for personal development.

Years ago, however, many people would attend classes because they had to, and personal growth was viewed very differently. In those days, most people would put paperwork in a drawer and do little with it. However, today is incredibly different, and the epidemic has enabled us to do things quite differently.

We discovered that the optimum training is a blend of online and in-person classes. A face-to-face training course—not just any old course or off-the-shelf course —but one that is tailored to the organisation and delivers exactly what they require.

We also favour short, concentrated videos of no more than five minutes due to individuals' lower concentration spans. We have found that adding a community then puts the learning into practice, reinforced by online group coaching calls, allowing users to communicate, and engage with others on the same learning growth path. This, without a doubt, is a mix that works for all generations.

If there's one thing to take away from this chapter, and even to start implementing, it is the necessity of personal growth, as well as the awareness of the importance that Generation Z places on this matter, to be taken for granted.

While we understand that this is a shorter chapter than our others, we hope that you received it well and will be able to apply and adapt it, because implementing personal development as a vital aspect of every organisation will not only attract Generation Z, but also other talent from other generations who will see the same emphasis and importance of holistic individual growth.

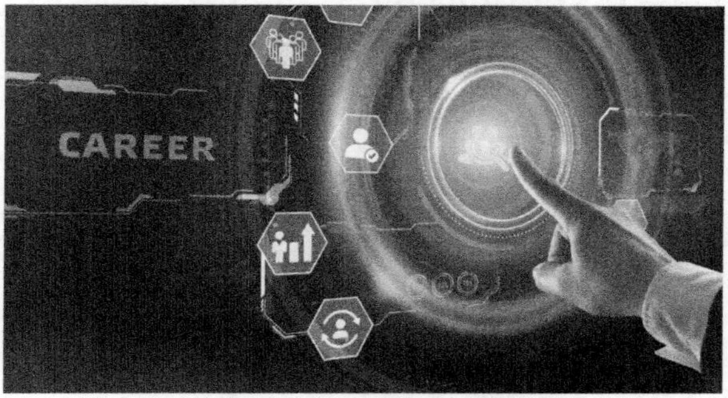

15

THE IMPORTANCE OF DIVERSITY AND INCLUSION

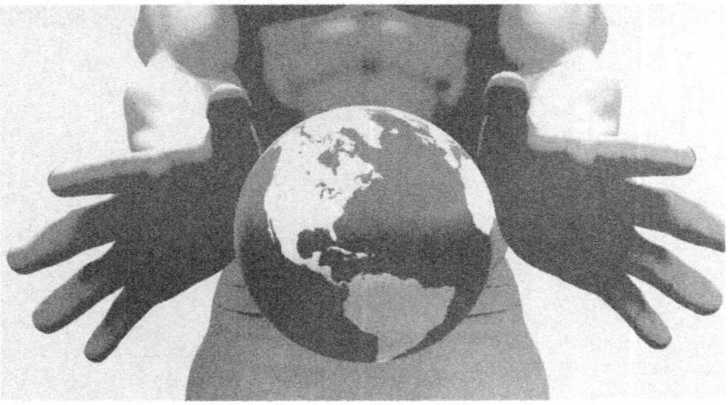

Diversity and inclusivity are important to Generation Z.

The first question we need to ask ourselves is why this is so important to them, and how it differs from previous generations.

In this chapter, we will cover diversity and inclusion

in greater depth, but rather than defining these issues, we will look at how Generation Z perceives them, and why they are such crucial elements for any company today.

In today's increasingly diversified business environment, people should understand what diversity and inclusion mean. That's not what we're going to discuss in this chapter. Instead, we'll look at how Generation Z has grown up in an increasingly varied environment, and how they see these issues as important to their lives, and interactions.

Generation Z fully understands that diversity significantly impacts innovation, creativity, and decision-making. We believe this is valid.

When you think about how far we have come as a human race in just the last few years, it is clear how immense diversity has become, and how imperative it is, for all of us to consider diversity, a critical point in every organisation.

Perhaps for this reason, Generation Z considers this area to be non-negotiable in work. Old-school managers and leaders must be well conscious of this. This is critical to winning over Generation Z, and it should not be viewed as an optional exercise.

We suggest that you give this the utmost attention, and really make it a part of the business, before Generation Z stops caring about their job, and doubts their role in the organisation.

GENERATION Z SEES diversity and equality as essential, to building a fair society. Not only do they view these as necessary for a fair society, but they also see organisations with values, and an emphasis on equality, as the most aligned with their values.

In all actuality, these organisations that emphasise equality, and promote the inclusive environments that Generation Z seeks, will be the ones who maintain Generation Z workers for the long term.

Without a doubt, institutions and businesses have gone above and beyond to promote justice and equality in recent years. Organisations value diversity and appreciate individuals who bring unique perspectives to the table.

Many businesses have recognised the significance of this, and how they can use it to drive innovative change, and improve their organisations from the inside out.

To put it another way, if your organisation has significant gaps in terms of diversity and inclusion, Generation Z is more inclined to engage in activism, lobby for policies and practices, and even demand tremendous and often revolutionary change.

We should not forget that they are extremely vocal on social media platforms, so if your company lacks diversity and inclusion, they are more likely to share it with their peers.

This is all caused by a combination of factors, and ultimately, Group Think, which we have discussed before. This is rooted in affinity bias, and social media pressure; much of this is essential in understanding Generation Z, and how they view diversity and inclusion.

These members of Generation Z will have such strong feelings about certain aspects of these topics, including diversity, that they will express their opinions. This may eventually lead to the development of a poor reputation for your organisation, if it is constantly being criticised, by employees from Generation Z. This can be all down to the fact that the business does not emphasise diversity and inclusion. Therefore, the consequences can be significant from a business point of view.

PREVIOUS GENERATIONS WOULD RECALL widespread discrimination. We know from our day that this area of attention was monumental, thus we believe this current shift towards inclusivity is amazing. You must understand that our generation entered the workforce in the late 1970s and early 1980s, and what is happening now is quite different from what happened when we were younger.

There was no discussion of diversity, equality, or inclusion back then. Now things are completely different. Generation Z is quite vocal about how all of these areas affect people's daily lives, resulting in substantial differences in how diversity and inclusion are perceived compared to 50 years earlier.

There is a massive difference in how they view the government as well, because they are known for being so much more involved, and even more of a generation of activists, than some of the older generations.

Generation Z is known to care significantly more about social issues, and are more likely to believe that the government should do more, to solve the problems. They think this is the right direction rather than businesses, or individuals, seeking collective action, instead of individual changes that create a ripple effect over a more extended period.

The fact that 59% of members of Generation Z believe that more gender options should be included on forms, is one issue to take into consideration. They feel that there should be even more alternatives for individuals, to genuinely portray who they are as individuals.

In another study, 83% of Generation Z individuals

stated that an employer's commitment to diversity, and inclusion, is significant when they choose a place to work. In another poll, we found that 75% of people in Generation Z, said they would consider applying for a job at another company, if they weren't satisfied with the diversity, or inclusion efforts, at their current place.

This is considerably different from other generations and moreover, demonstrates the significance of ensuring that organisations are well prepared, diverse, inclusive, and accepting of all individuals. Not taking this into account, and you may struggle to keep Generation Z workers, who will become the majority in just a few years. Just think how much this costs the organisation.

THE FACTS REVEALED on Generation Z's affinity for diversity and inclusion demonstrate how much more significant this is than we might assume. Generation Z supports diversity and inclusivity, and there is a wealth of more information on the Internet concerning this topic.

There was one quote that we found that we genuinely liked, and it's the following:

"Diversity is being invited to the party, and inclusion is being asked to dance."

Such a simple, and effective quote, genuinely exemplifies what Generation Z wants in organisations, and how they can respond.

We have used this quote when talking to older generations, discussing how diversity and inclusion can be integrated into the workplace, or any organisation.

Generation Z appreciates the community of diverse people who mutually support, and respect each other, despite any differences that they may have. \

We know first-hand how important it is to learn to understand the people around you, but Generation Z thinks and feels in a more diverse way than many.

WHY NOT ASK yourself these three critical questions:

1. Is everyone treated equally in our workplace?
2. What can I do to be more inclusive?
3. Are everyone's opinions considered equally?

THESE ANSWERS CAN SHARE a lot about the organisation's current state of diversity and inclusion.

Then, make sure you ask yourself one final, critical question of inquiry:

4. What could I do differently, and how can I think differently?

We don't believe anyone can answer these questions perfectly, and we don't expect people to always prioritise this area before examining these concerns.

We have found that people don't really prioritise this area. However, just thinking about this chapter alone, we should all think more about diversity and inclusion, and how we can improve this area personally and professionally.

For instance, consider education on this subject: what have you done to understand this area?

Let us be honest: equality and diversity can be mocked by the other generations. They say they believe in it, but their actions speak something completely different, and it's very noticeable.

Have you put yourself in adverse situations, to help your understanding further?

Have you updated your knowledge?

Are you truly investing in your education and

allowing yourself to cultivate an understanding of those around you, from diverse populations?

Furthermore, did you know that a study found that teams comprised of individuals, from varied backgrounds, surpass teams made up entirely of similar members, by as much as 87% in performance for business?

Yes 87%, which is huge.

Remember that real teams thrive from true diversity. It's more than just race or religion variety. There are many different types of people who can benefit your team. This includes people from various backgrounds, experience levels, and sectors. Diversity is more than just the visual aspects that some people discuss; it goes far deeper.

As a recruiter in the 1980s for the Royal Air Force, we had to ensure we had recruited a certain quota from non-white backgrounds. However, although the question was asked, if we are honest, no one ever took that question seriously.

Now, times have certainly changed considerably, but you can see how diversity has evolved, and how we can all include more diverse populations in our organisations.

Now, times have certainly changed considerably, but you can see how diversity has evolved, and how we can all include more diverse populations in our organisations.

It is incredible to learn that diverse teams have an easier time with efficiency and productivity up to 87 percent of the time. Real diversity is a lot more complicated than it appears to be at first glance. As was indicated before, our outward appearance is only one aspect of our diversity; yet, the diversity that exists among us extends far further than that.

When individuals with diverse backgrounds get to know each other by working together, more solutions are inevitably presented, and decisions can be made with even better perspectives than before.

We have found this in nearly all of our training, regardless of the course. So, if your organisation implements good diversity and inclusion tactics, Generation Z will undoubtedly notice.

Then you must assess what opportunities this creates for you within your business. Consider how many more initiatives will come from such various backgrounds.

From an organisational standpoint, your workplace will become an even more appealing place to work.

Particularly among younger generations that value the diversity and inclusivity that you have promoted, implemented, and even integrated into your organisation.

Sometimes, it is good to remember where it all started. The demands for equal rights for all, regardless of race, gender, or ethnicity, led the way to such significant emphasis on diversity and inclusion. In the many decades that followed this, since diversity and inclusion have become priorities, these topics have become increasingly important within the workplace. We would have never thought about it years ago, but now, here we are.

We do not doubt, that sharp businesses globally have realised the importance of diversity and inclusion. They understand how important this area is, and how having an inclusive workforce is essential for their success, now, and in the long term.

We think the training regarding diversity and inclusion that came at the start was probably not the best.

In our opinion, having a simple tick box to show that you followed a simple program is obviously rubbish.

Let's face it: tick-box exercises for diversity and inclusion were and still are complete rubbish.

They don't educate you in any way, and even then, poor training does nothing but hinder your education.

This only fuels the cynics to become more cynical, making those hopeful even more disengaged, and unattached to the work they complete in the organisation.

Even more noteworthy, is the hindered progress due to the challenges Generation Z continues to face. However, every generation has to encounter struggles, and doubts, when they join the workforce.

We must remember that Generation Z entered the workforce during a global pandemic, with fears of inflation rates, recession fears, global conflicts, and climate change. Furthermore, as we keep saying, excessive debt from universities.

These are undoubtedly several concerns compared to what we had growing up in our era.

In our era, there were always jobs, and everybody left school around the age of 16. Only 3% of people went to college, or university, as we discussed before, and straight away, you were encouraged to think about pensions and mortgages.

We had no debt like today's youngsters, nothing to their scale. We grew up in the Cold War era, a far different story, but a safer and more consistent world in other ways.

That is likely why Generation Z are more likely to have an independent job, or even multiple jobs, more so than the older workers. They have a completely different philosophy regarding work and their life, and it shows, based on our observations and the research we have found.

Generation Z is much more likely to report that their pay does not allow them to have a good quality of life. Are you aware that there are concerning levels of stress among young people. This includes an astounding 55%, who report either having been diagnosed with, or having received treatment for mental illness?

On top of this, to give you an idea, only 31% of people aged 55 to 64 have reported the same conditions. This is a huge difference, so it's important to reflect on this, and recognise the significant number of challenges, that Generation Z faces, compared to where we are today.

All those years ago, when we were younger, would you ever imagine a situation?

We know it was never educated the same way, as mental health issues are more seriously taken today than they were before. There were some serious mental

health issues then, but they were vastly different.

So, when you find yourself irritated or frustrated, because some of your younger generation staff are wandering around with headphones, or saying they are going for a silent walk (headphones out).

Take a moment and think about what we have covered. Think about how they see the world, and what they are facing, and how we can learn to communicate better and celebrate everybody's diversity.

Just think about this chapter and the learning that can come if you truly reflect on your reactions and biases.

What biases are you carrying today?

How can you lead yourself and your organisation towards including or integrating diversity and equality?

THE ISSUE, quite honestly, is possibly you, but there's nowhere to go but up from here, as there are many ways that you can improve this in the future. See this a beginning for change both personally, and professionally.

. . .

To HELP, just ask yourself some of these questions:

- Are you authentic?
- What have you verbally mentioned in conversations?
- Are you inclusive?
- How updated are your systems to include D&I?
- How are you with environmental issues?
- Have you disregarded environmental concerns?
- Who is the group of people in your inner circle, diverse?
- What is your culture really like?
- What is your communication style? (Gen Z hates overly formal or bureaucratic communication)
- Do you respect other's privacy?

BE sure to be honest with yourself about the answers to these questions.

These are some great questions to think about, and if you allow yourself to be honest, you can start to think about the changes you can make that will make even more improvements in the organisations you are a part of.

We do hope this chapter helped you reflect on this area. The differences you may see in yourself compared to Generation Z.

If anything, this chapter truly displays the importance of diversity and inclusion and how we all can focus on truly recognising and supporting each other while also seeking even more understanding about how we differ as demographics.

16

SUMMARY

As we finish our discussion on Generation Z, there's plenty to think about for the future, regardless of what industry you may work in.

The insights that we have provided in this book are not just for those in business, but in any organisation today, as our workforce continues to diversify to new and exciting levels.

From communication to motivation, as well as mentoring and reverse mentoring for this demographic, we have covered a plethora of topics, that will undoubtedly be useful for any professional in today's world.

However, we want to impress upon you, the importance of recognising that what we have shared is merely our own understanding of Generation Z.

The views that we have expressed are our own, based on what we have observed from the many hours that we have spent in the training rooms and coaching relationships, workplaces, and out in public settings.

Generation Z are not all going to appear as we have described, but it is important that we reflect on our own individual experiences. There may be some commonalities, but as you navigate the workplace, and how you associate with this growing demographic, you'll come to find that nearly every single individual is unique, and has their own strengths. This is precisely why we wrote this book, after all: to explore how we can manage, support, and strengthen Generation Z to become the next generation of leaders.

As we have engaged with various individuals from Generation Z, and have been enlightened as we learned more about their perspectives, it has been incredibly enriching for us as Baby Boomers.

We have learned a vast amount from those with whom we have interacted and feel that we have gained valuable insights that have supported all of our views in this book, not just on Generation Z but from all ends of the generational spectrum.

In sharing our diverse perspectives, we hope to have enlightened you and allowed you to think more critically about how we all can find commonality in each other.

While our exploration solely focused on Generation Z in this text, we hope to cover other similar generations in future books. Discovering all that we can about today's generations is paramount for our success in any industry.

Of course what is coming next is Generation Alpha, these are individuals born from 2010 to 2024, which will be a whole new dynamic to add to the equation. Who knows what else we have yet to uncover about today's society?

We hope to broaden our investigation beyond Generation Z as our world continues to evolve and transform. And so do the expectations that we must set, and what we can do as professionals, to assist the next generation when they enter the workforce.

Throughout our chapters, we have delved deep into everything related to Generation Z within the workplace. We have explored their worldview and the importance of diversity and globalisation to their scope of work, and how they live their life.

We have also given an in-depth exploration into how they work and their work ethic, allowing us all to reflect on where they divert and remain similar to us in the office. In other sections, we highlighted their increasingly noticeable entrepreneurial spirit and how much they are driven by the pursuit of their own individual goals. Finally, we also ensured that we touched upon the importance of social change to them, as it remains a firm commitment—both personally and professionally—that guides them in their decision-making and their consumerism.

The changes ahead in our world are unmistakable, particularly in how we must educate the older generations. As Baby Boomers, we have seen the disruptions and shifts that are happening and how much our world is transforming right before our eyes. In our opinion, the only pathway forward for the future is to adapt our management and leadership styles. If we do not, we cannot leverage and benefit from the power of Generation Z, and their uniqueness.

As one of the most technologically savvy and socially committed generations, not only are their diverse traits something to appreciate, but they are an opportunity for us to learn why these values matter, and how we can innovate with the help of the newest innovations.

Transformation is imperative for us all to navigate the challenges that lie ahead, and even the ones that exist today. If we do not take advantage of what Generation Z has to share with us, we might miss out on the critical opportunities that will help us work with technology and build a more socially conscious world.

As we continue to lead and manage our teams, let us not forget the importance of adaptation. Even if our ways were the best long ago, that is not the case today. Together, we can pave a different, collaborative path for the future that honours what Generation Z has to offer, while keeping the very best of what we have cultivated, as leaders and veterans of the industries.

We were inspired to write this book for more than one reason. In the first place, we wanted to really deal with the misunderstanding that many people in Generation Z have. People have only thought of Generation Z as a group, who are hooked on their phones.

This included us, and if we are honest, we held a bias that we now realise was wrong.

As a society, we haven't taken enough of a chance to understand them, their problems, and why they behave the way they do.

We wrote this book to argue against the common view that Generation Z needs to change. Instead, we wanted to show the many ways we think they excel, and could make the world a better place.

Furthermore, we wished to educate those who aren't sure how to deal with Generation Z in work settings. As trainers and coaches, we have been blessed with the opportunity to work with so many professionals, in helping them become better managers and leaders.

We saw that many people didn't know how to work with Generation Z, which was sad to see since we were helping to bring about big changes in many fields and businesses. When it comes to working with Generation Z, the mix of misunderstandings and confusion is not helpful.

In a workplace where managers and leaders don't know how to work with a specific demographic, this leads to alienation and challenges in the workplace. Employees that simply cannot mesh with the rest.

It is our firm belief that traditional management and leadership courses often overlook the need for collaboration among different generations. Too often, they attempt to reduce the practice of management and the study of leadership to a standardised approach. This then fails to take into account the diversity of today's workforce.

Therefore, we wanted to provide a more comprehensive, digestible book that would give you a clear look at Generation Z and a tailored approach to working with this unique Generation. After all, there is no one-size-fits-all approach when it comes to leading others. We must all do our part to tailor our support to each, and every employee, by understanding their individuality and how they work.

We believe that it is absolutely crucial for us to bridge the gap in management training. We need to properly understand how we can all work together, specifically providing guidance in the realm of induction processes, reverse mentoring, and managing up, as we discussed.

If we learn more about these vital areas, we can continue to support the next generation of leaders that we will find in Generation Z. Not only that, but we can also learn along the way, too.

With reverse mentoring, all of the technological tools that we struggle with—us included as Baby Boomers—can become more apparent, and we can get firm guidance from those, like Generation Z, who understand how to use these resources to improve their production and efficiency.

By managing up our Generation Z workers, we can also find ways to help them become more involved, tapping into their great desire for mentorship, and one-on-one coaching, that we have explored in this book. As you can see, we can bridge this gap with management training, and we should.

Not just so that, we feel comfortable leaving our organisations in good hands, but also, so that we show Generation Z more about our values, and what they can take with them into the future, as they lead our industries and countries.

As we wrote this book, we often reflected on our son Jack's experiences, as well as what we learned in the management training courses that we have led over the years. Our son is a fellow Generation Z himself and has taught us a great deal about all that his generation cares about.

In many ways, our own observations in this book also come from what we know about Jack, and his values! However, we also had to stop and reflect on our own courses, and what we taught. In doing so, we realise now, as we close out our book, that many share similar concerns about effectively engaging Generation Z in the workforce, as we have expressed in this book.

People are concerned about how to reach Generation Z, how to encourage their collaboration, and how we can all work together more cohesively and on the same page. And we understand—we shared some of the same concerns, too. We have experienced these same concerns ourselves, as we network and collaborate with others in our field, even globally.

Our hope is that our book gives you some hope and some insight into how we can manage this new generation, and what benefits some of these ideas will have in encouraging not only your success, but also your success as a professional leader or manager.

Moving forward, practical application is a must. We cannot just take these lessons and do nothing with them, but we must find ways to implement them in our lives. For those who manage and lead companies, do not be afraid to find new ways to communicate with your employees or even establish new protocols for evaluation of where you can change.

As professionals and trainers, we look forward to reshaping our management and leadership training. We hope to continue to refine our own training, to integrate the insights and findings that we have provided in this book, but we hope that you also do the same.

In your companies, be sure to implement some of these tips and lessons that we have shared to update your policies, training, and more. It's essential that we continue to enhance what we do, and how we support our young workers.

If we want to see even further success in our efforts —regardless of our company's size—we must find ways to nurture and retain talent. It is not enough anymore to simply follow the old ways; we must create new transformative pathways, that challenge us all to become better as leaders and professionals.

If we want to progress in our companies and industries, we must also be willing to progress individually, starting with how we see the world, and how much change we are eager to accept in our own lives. All the critical change begins within, as I am sure you have gathered from all we have discussed!

As you find new ways to implement some of these findings in your organisations, don't be afraid to ask for some insight from your Generation Z counterparts. Ask them how they would feel about specific changes, and don't forget to ensure that they would benefit from what you are about to offer or alter. Above all else, as you seek insight and guidance, mutual and collective benefit should be at the forefront.

We have no doubt that companies that will find ways to make these changes will see drastic impacts for the better, in their work, and their future levels of success. As trainers, we have already heard from so many who have attended our courses, that they have experienced massive metamorphoses in their own companies.

They have watched disengaged workers become invested even more in their projects. Many have even reported inter-generational collaboration—a true must-have in any organisation, in our opinion, for the future.

All of this could be your organisation's reality, if you're willing to make the changes to support a different future for us all as professionals, no matter what industry you're in.

As long as we find ways to collaborate and leverage our shared and distinct strengths, every generation can succeed and move forward with confidence into our increasingly technological future. The hardest part of ensuring this change, is making the decision to think differently and to adapt, as we all must.

We hope that this book has provided you with some

valuable insights and has inspired you to think bigger about the change you could enact in your organisation. It's not enough these days to stick to the same old tried and tested methods. It's time for us all to think outside the box. These insights could be the catalyst for positive change in your organisation, and even in your workplace dynamics.

If you struggle with team members who cannot collaborate and cannot understand how to work together, this book can help you bridge the gaps or, at the very least, know why they persist.

Together, we can embrace the opportunity to communicate and collaborate effectively with Generation Z. Whether you're a Baby Boomer, Generation X, Millennial, or Generation Z yourself, we all have an opportunity to move forward together with shared values that can shape the future.

If we all focus on how we can incorporate Generation Z more adequately into the workplace, to cultivate their leadership and development, then we all can enrich our businesses and foster mutual growth, that will create a ripple effect around the world.

We have the power to change the future of work, and we hope that you join us in this initiative. As trainers, nothing brings us greater joy than seeing organisations and leaders transform, step up to the challenge, and truly work to pave a pathway for a beneficial future for all.

Thank you for reading and learning about the power of Generation Z and how we can manage them more effectively because they are the future.

Warmest Regards,

Claire and Ralph Moody

For more information on our courses and resources, please visit our website: www.targettrg.co.uk

AFTERWORD

Enjoy this guide? You can make a big difference

Reviews are the most powerful tool in our arsenal when it comes to getting attention for our guides and journals. Much as we would like to, we don't have the big bucks of a New York Publisher to throw at advertising in Time Square. Well not yet anyway!

But we do have something with a more powerful punch than that, the ultimate weapon, something those publishers would love to get their hands on.

A committed and loyal bunch of readers. You are our weapons of mass distribution (WMD).

Honest reviews of our books help bring them to the attention of other readers.

If you enjoyed this book, we would be very grateful if you could spend just five minutes leaving a review (it can be as short as you like). Just visit the amazon site and click on review this book.

Thank you very much.

Claire and Ralph

ABOUT THE AUTHORS

Claire and Ralph Moody have over 40 years of experience in developing people across the globe. Owners of a world-class training and coaching company, Target Training Associates.

Their company specialises in trainer, coach, leadership and management development, and they offer courses to a worldwide audience.

Their biggest achievement is when individuals make significant improvements in their lives.

Using their expertise in training, coaching and mentoring, they have adapted the journaling technique with fantastic results. Being keen writers themselves and having experienced how powerful a great book can be in personal development, they wanted to share the experience with a broader audience and subject areas.

They live and have offices in London and have one son (Jack) who still enjoys his parents' company, especially if they are paying!

As a family, they live life to the full and enjoy aviation and travel.

As a couple and self-starters themselves, they have developed significantly over the years and have vast experience which they are keen to share for others to build on.

Printed in Great Britain
by Amazon

40738256R00159